Lonely  planet

POCKET

WASHINGTON

TOP EXPERIENCES · LOCAL LIFE

T0022840

KARLA ZIMMERMAN

Contents

Plan Your Trip 4

Top Experiences 4

Dining Out..........................10

Museums &
Monuments 12

For Kids 14

Bar Open 16

Treasure Hunt 17

Live Music 18

For Free 19

LGBTIQ+ 20

Theater &
Performing Arts 21

Art & Architecture 22

History & Politics 23

Under the Radar
Washington, DC 24

Active DC 25

Four Perfect Days.............26

Need to Know 28

Washington, DC
Neighborhoods 30

The Vietnam Veterans Memorial (p38)
DESIGNER: MAYA LIN. IMAGE: JAN VAN DASLER/SHUTTERSTOCK ©

Explore
Washington, DC 33

National Mall 35

**White House area
and Foggy Bottom** 57

Georgetown 71

Capitol Hill 81

**Downtown, Penn Quarter
& Logan Circle** 97

Dupont Circle 115

Adams Morgan 129

Special Features

Lincoln Memorial 36

Vietnam Veterans
Memorial 38

Washington
Monument 40

National Air &
Space Museum 42

US Capitol 82

The Declaration of
Independence 98

Arlington National
Cemetery 139

Survival
Guide 141

Before You Go 142

Arriving in DC 143

Getting Around 144

Essential Information 145

Index 151

COVID-19

We have re-checked every business in this book before publication to ensure that it is still open after the COVID-19 outbreak. However, the economic and social impacts of COVID-19 will continue to be felt long after the outbreak has been contained, and many businesses, services and events referenced in this guide may experience ongoing restrictions. Some businesses may be temporarily closed, have changed their opening hours and services, or require bookings; some unfortunately could have closed permanently. We suggest you check with venues before visiting for the latest information.

Washington, DC's Top Experiences

Admire the Lincoln Memorial (p36)

CAAMALF/SHUTTERSTOCK ©

Enjoy sweeping views from
the Washington Monument (p40)

Reflect and Remember at the Vietnam Veterans Memorial (p38)

DESIGNER: MAYA LIN. IMAGE: S.F/SHUTTERSTOCK ©

See the Declaration of Independence at the National Archives (p98)

UNGVAR/SHUTTERSTOCK ©

POPOVA VALERIYA/SHUTTERSTOCK ©

Take in the Grandeur of the US Capitol (p82)

Let Your Mind Take Flight at the National Air and Space Museum (p42)

KARINA EREMINA/SHUTTERSTOCK ©

Visit the President at the White House (p58)

Absorb History at the Holocaust Memorial Museum (p84)

Visit JFK's Grave at Arlington National Cemetery (p139)

VICTOR LAFUENTE ALONSO/SHUTTERSTOCK ©

CHRISTIAN HINKLE/SHUTTERSTOCK ©

Be Awed at the Reynolds Center for American Art & Portraiture (p100)

Dining Out

A homegrown foodie revolution has transformed the once-buttoned-up DC dining scene. Driving it is the bounty of farms on its doorstep, a booming local economy and its worldly young residents. Small, local-chef-helmed spots now lead the way. And they're doing such a fine job that Michelin deemed the city worthy of its stars.

Global Influence

Washington, DC, is one of the most international cities in America, heavily populated by immigrants, expats and diplomats from all over the world. People crave the food of home, and so there's a glut of great international eating. Salvadoran, Ethiopian, Vietnamese, French, Spanish, West African – they've all become Washingtonian.

Local Bounty

The city's unique geography puts it between two of the best food-production areas in America: Chesapeake Bay and the Virginia Piedmont. From the former come crabs, oysters and rockfish; the latter provides game, pork, wine and peanuts. Chefs take advantage of this delicious abundance, and the accolades follow.

Southern Influence

Keep in mind that DC occupies the fault line between two of America's greatest culinary regions: the Northeast and the South. The city offers heaps of soul food and its high-class incarnations, so get ready for plates of fried chicken, catfish, collard greens, sweet-potato hash and butter-smothered grits.

Best for Foodies

Dabney Rustic room cooking up overlooked mid-Atlantic flavors. (p106)

Tail Up Goat Mediterranean shared plates in breezy, island-like environs. (p131)

Rose's Luxury Worth the wait for worldly comfort food and friendly service. (p87)

Best Budget

Donburi Fifteen seats at the counter for authentic Japanese rice bowls. (p131)

JON HICKS/GETTY IMAGES ©

Simply Banh Mi Vietnamese pho and lemongrass pork sandwiches. (p77)

Best Local

Ben's Chili Bowl Gossip with locals while downing a half-smoke. (p113; pictured)

Bistrot du Coin Hearty French fare from steak *frites* to mussels. (p117)

Best Vegetarian

Chorohe Ethiopian stews in a colorful townhouse. (p106)

Shouk Bright-tiled eatery for vegan Israeli food. (p107)

Best Seafood

Maine Avenue Fish Market Shrimp, crabs and oysters fried, broiled or steamed. (p92)

Fiola Mare Georgetown's river-view hot spot delivers an Italian twist. (p77)

Best Sweets

Baked & Wired DC's biggest and bestest cupcakes. (p73)

Un Je Ne Sais Quoi French pastries piled high. (p122)

Best Brunch

Ted's Bulletin Sink into a retro booth for beer biscuits and house-made pop tarts. (p92)

Diner Scarf omelets, berry pancakes and Bloody Marys 24/7. (p132)

Worth a Trip: Eat the World

Chowhounds hobnob at **Union Market** (www.unionmarketdc.com; 1309 5th St NE; mains $6-11; ⊙11am-8pm Tue-Fri, from 8am Sat & Sun; Ⓜ Red Line to NoMa), a sunlit warehouse-turned-food-hall where culinary entrepreneurs sell everything from Burmese milkshakes to Korean tacos.

Museums & Monuments

There's nothing quite like the Smithsonian Institution, a collection of 19 artifact-stuffed museums, many lined up in a row along the Mall. Rockets, dinosaurs, Warhol paintings – even the 45-carat Hope Diamond lights up a room. Washington's monuments – potent symbols of the nation's history and its makers – add to the stockpile.

Smithsonian Stash

Thanks, James Smithson, you eccentric anti-monarchist Englishman. That $508,318 gift you willed to the USA back in 1829 to create a 'diffusion of knowledge' paid off. The Smithsonian holds 156 million artworks, scientific specimens, artifacts and other objects in its trove of museums, and they're all free.

Other Museums & Exhibits

DC has many more museums beyond the Smithsonian. Freebies include the National Gallery of Art and United States Holocaust Memorial Museum. The National Archives and Library of Congress aren't technically museums, but they hold museum-caliber exhibits. There are also a handful of admission-charging entities.

Monument Madness

Monuments are so prevalent you'd think it'd be easy to get one built. Not so. First you need Congressional approval. Then you have to raise a *lot* of money and get everyone to agree on a design. Take the Martin Luther King Jr Memorial. The idea had been floating around for decades. Congress approved it in 1996; $120 million and 15 years later, it finally opened in 2011.

Best Science Museums

National Air and Space Museum Rockets, missiles and the biplane. (p42)

National Museum of Natural History Gems, minerals, mummies and a giant squid. (p49)

MICHAEL HARE/SHUTTERSTOCK ©

Best History Museums

United States Holocaust Memorial Museum Brutal and impassioned exhibits about the millions murdered by the Nazis. (p84)

National Museum of African American History and Culture A powerful collection with Harriet Tubman's hymnal, Emmett Till's casket and more. (p48)

National Museum of American History Everything from a piece of Plymouth Rock to Dorothy's ruby slippers. (p49)

Best Art Museums

Reynolds Center for American Art & Portraiture Portraits on one side,

O'Keeffe, Hopper and more on the other. (p100)

National Gallery of Art It takes two massive buildings to hold all the art. (p49)

Best Monuments

Lincoln Memorial Abe Lincoln gazes across the Mall from his Doric-columned temple. (p36; pictured)

Vietnam Veterans Memorial The black wall

reflects the names of the Vietnam War's 58,300-plus casualties. (p38)

Martin Luther King Jr Memorial Dr King's 30ft-tall likeness emerges from a mountain of granite. (p48)

Washington Monument The iconic obelisk, DC's tallest structure, offers unparalleled views from the top. (p40)

Top Tips

○ Most monuments are open 24/7 and are particularly atmospheric in the morning or lit up at night.

○ Timed-entry tickets are needed for major monuments. You can preorder online.

For Kids

Elephants: Big Bodies, Big Impacts

Washington bursts with kid-friendly attractions. Not only does it hold the nation's best collection of dinosaur bones, rockets and one-of-a-kind historical artifacts, but just about everything is free. Another bonus: green space surrounds all the sights, so young ones can burn off energy to their hearts' content.

Advance Reservations

Some sights – including the International Spy Museum, National Archives, Washington Monument, Ford's Theatre and the Capitol – allow you to make advance reservations for a small fee. During peak season (late March through August), it pays to go online and do so up to a month prior to avoid lengthy queues.

Rainy-Day Options

The Smithsonian has two Imax theaters on the Mall: one in the National Museum of Natural History, and the other in the National Air and Space Museum. The latter also holds the Einstein Planetarium. Schedules are amalgamated at www.si.edu/imax.

Films to Set the Mood

In *Night at the Museum 2: Battle of the Smithsonian* (2009), museum exhibits come to life for Ben Stiller in the National Air and Space Museum and National Gallery of Art. (FYI, the first film was set in New York City's American Museum of Natural History, and the third film takes place at London's British Museum.)

In *National Treasure* (2004) Nicolas Cage finds a coded map on the back of the Declaration of Independence that leads to – that's right – national treasure!

Best Museums

National Museum of Natural History The mummified kitty, T. rex skull and tarantula feedings generate big squeals. (p49; pictured)

National Air and Space Museum Touch moon rocks and walk through space capsules. (p42)

KIT LEONG/SHUTTERSTOCK ©

National Museum of American History Gawp at the Star-Spangled Banner flag, and George Washington's sword. (p49)

National Building Museum Seek out the Building Zone to stack block towers and drive toy bulldozers. (p104)

Best Entertainment

National Theatre Free Saturday morning performances, from puppet shows to tap dancers. (p111)

Discovery Theater The Smithsonian's kids' theater features cultural plays and storytelling. (p53)

Georgetown Waterfront Park Splash in the fountains and curlicue through the maze. (p73)

Best Kids' Cuisine

Diner Drawing materials for kids, booze for parents, 24-hour service and American food classics for all. (p132)

Ted's Bulletin Retro spot serving smiley-face pancakes and peanut-butter-and-jelly sandwiches. (p92)

Best Shops

International Spy Museum The shop carries everything from mustache disguises to voice-changing gadgets. (p104)

Tugooh Toys Wood blocks, ecofriendly stuffed animals and educational games line the shelves. (p79)

Top Tips

o Most museums provide family guide booklets with activities kids can do on site.

o DC Cool Kids (www.washington.org/dc-cool-kids) features activity guides and insider tips from local youngsters on things to do.

Bar Open

When Andrew Jackson swore the oath of office in 1829, the self-proclaimed populist dispensed with pomp and threw a raging kegger. Folks got so gone they started looting art from the White House. The historical lesson: DC loves a drink, and these days it enjoys said tipples in many incarnations besides executive-mansion-trashing parties.

SCOTT SUCHMAN/FOR THE WASHINGTON POST/GETTY IMAGES ©

Best Cocktails

Copycat Co Fizzy cocktails in welcoming, opium den environs. (p93)

Bar Charley Friendly Dupont spot that mixes drinks in vintage glassware. (p123)

Best Beer

Bluejacket Brewery Sour blonds to barley wines made on-site. (p93; pictured)

Churchkey 500 different beers, including 50 craft brews on tap. (p108)

Best Clubs

U Street Music Hall Casual, DJ-owned spot to get your dance on. (p113)

18th Street Lounge Sexy young things groove in a Dupont mansion. (p124)

Best Dives

Dan's Cafe It's like an evil Elks Club, with massive pours of booze. (p134)

Tune Inn Ah, beer swilled under mounted deer heads. (p87)

Best Local Scene

Right Proper Brewing Co House-made ales flow in Duke Ellington's old pool hall. (p113)

Wonderland Ballroom Edgy, eccentric, with oddball folk art and outdoor picnic tables for mingling. (p137)

Board Room Knock back draft beers and crush your opponent at Battleship, Operation and other classic board games. (p117)

Top Tip

○ Washington is a big happy-hour town. Practically all bars have some sort of drink and/or food special for a few hours between 4pm and 7pm.

Treasure Hunt

Shopping in DC means many things, from browsing funky antique shops to perusing rare titles at secondhand booksellers. Temptations abound for lovers of vinyl, vintage wares, and one-of-a-kind jewelry, art, and handicrafts. And, of course, that Abe Lincoln pencil sharpener and Uncle Sam bobblehead you've been waiting for...

KARINA MOVSESYAN/SHUTTERSTOCK ©

Best Markets

Eastern Market Butcher, baker and blue-crab maker on weekdays, plus artisans and farmers on weekends. (p87)

Flea Market Weekend browser for cool art, furniture, clothing, global wares and bric-a-brac. (p87)

Best Antiques

Book Hill Galleries, interior design stores and antique shops all in a row in Georgetown. (p71)

Best Books

Capitol Hill Books So many volumes; they're even for sale in the bathroom. (p87)

Second Story Books Antiquarian books and old sheet music, plus cheap sidewalk bins to rummage in. (p125)

Kramerbooks New books on the shelves, hearty food in the cafe, happening into the wee hours. (p117; pictured)

Idle Time Books Great political and history stacks among the three creaky floors of used tomes. (p135)

Best Souvenirs

White House Gifts Presidential golf balls, T-shirts, snow globes: a quintessential spot for goofy DC trinkets. (p69)

National Archives Peruse the Archives Shop for when you need a Declaration-inscribed ruler or John Adams stuffed toy. (p98)

Best Fashion

Meeps Cowboy shirts, Jackie O sunglasses and magnificent duds from past eras. (p135)

CityCenterDC Glittery boutiques galore fill this shopping oasis. (p111)

Live Music

Washington's musical taste splits in several directions. Its jazz affair started in the early 20th century, when U St NW was known as Black Broadway for its slew of music theaters. Duke Ellington grew up in the neighborhood, and his influence lingers on. Blues, rock and global music also waft out of atmospheric local halls.

HOBERMAN COLLECTION/UNIVERSAL IMAGES GROUP VIA GETTY IMAGES ©

Neighborhood Hubs

Loads of clubs besides jazzy ones cluster around U St between 7th St and 14th St NW. The bands vary – alt-rock, hip-hop, soul, funk, Caribbean – but the common thread is that the venues are intimate, with something indie-cool going on. Other areas to scope out are H St NE in Capitol Hill for hip rock clubs, and 18th St NW in Adams Morgan for raucous music houses and world beats.

Best Rock, Funk & Blues

Hamilton Alt-rock and funk bands plug in a stone's throw from the White House. (p69)

Madam's Organ Prepare for wild times in Adams Morgan's bluesy hot spot. (p134; pictured)

Bukom Cafe Join the West African crowd getting their groove on to reggae beats. (p134)

Songbyrd Record Cafe Make your own record upstairs, then hear indie bands in the basement. (p134)

Best Jazz

Blues Alley Bringing in top names since Dizzy Gillespie's day. (p78)

Jazz in the Garden Tune in amid whimsical artworks in the National Sculpture Garden. (p53)

Howard Theatre Historic venue where Ella Fitzgerald once sang. (p113)

Top Tip

o See the alt-weekly *Washington City Paper* (www.washingtoncitypaper.com) for comprehensive listings.

For Free

Washington, DC, has a mind-blowing array of freebies. From the Smithsonian Institution's multiple museums, to gratis theater and concerts, to jaunts through the White House and Capitol, you can be entertained for weeks without spending a dime.

ANTON_IVANOV/SHUTTERSTOCK ©

Museum Mania

The Smithsonian Institution has an incredible bounty of free museums. Other free collections include the National Gallery of Art and the United States Holocaust Memorial Museum. Plus all of DC's monuments are free to visit. See Best Museums & Monuments for more.

Best Free Non-Museum Sights

National Archives Gape at the Declaration of Independence, Constitution and Bill of Rights. (p98)

Library of Congress The world's largest library displays centuries-old maps, bibles and Thomas Jefferson's books (p90)

Best Free Tours

White House Peek into the rooms of the President's abode. (p58)

Capitol Guides lead you through the white-domed sanctum of Congress, cluttered with statues and frescoes. (p82)

Ford's Theatre Explore the venue where John Wilkes Booth shot Abraham Lincoln. (p104)

Bureau of Engraving & Printing Watch millions of dollars get printed. (p91)

National Public Radio Wave to your favorite correspondents as you walk past the newsroom. (p91)

Best Free Entertainment

Kennedy Center The Millennium Stage hosts a free music or dance performance daily at 6pm. (p67; pictured)

Shakespeare Theatre Company Each August the troupe puts on a Bard classic for free. (p109)

Best Free Days at Paid Museums

Phillips Collection Free Tuesday through Friday for the permanent galleries. (p120)

National Museum of Women in the Arts Free the first Sunday of the month. (p105)

LGBTIQ+

RENA SCHILD/SHUTTERSTOCK ©

DC is one of the most gay-friendly cities in the US. It has an admirable track record of progressivism and a fair bit of scene to boot. The rainbow stereotype here consists of well-dressed professionals and activists working in politics on LGBTIQ+ issues such as gay marriage (legal in DC since 2010).

Neighborhood Hubs

The gay community concentrates in Dupont Circle. In recent years the party has spread toward Logan Circle, a short distance east. U Street, Shaw and Capitol Hill also have active scenes.

Events

The big event on the calendar is **Capital Pride** (www.capitalpride.org) in June. Some 250,000 people attend the gay pride party. The famed parade travels from Dupont Circle to Logan Circle. There's also **DC Black Pride** in late May.

Best for Fun

JR's Dupont pub where a young crowd kicks back and sings show tunes. (p117)

Larry's Lounge Neighborhood tavern that's perfect for people watching. (p123)

Perry's The restaurant's drag-queen Sunday brunch packs the house. (p132)

Dacha Beer Garden This outdoor spot becomes an unofficial gay hangout on Sundays. (p108)

Kramerbooks Bookstore and bistro that's open late night for heavy flirting. (p117)

Top Tips

∘ *Washington Blade* (www.washingtonblade.com) is a free weekly gay newspaper that covers politics, business and nightlife.

∘ *Metro Weekly* (www.metroweekly.com) is the younger rival weekly publication.

Theater & Performing Arts

MARK VAN SCYOC/SHUTTERSTOCK ©

Washington stages more than political theater. From the evening-wear elegance of the Kennedy Center to scrappy theater troupes in pubs, the nation's capital has an envious slate of performances. It caters to Shakespeare, classical-music and poetry-slam fans particularly well.

Best Theater

Shakespeare Theatre Company The nation's top troupe does the Bard proud. (p109)

Woolly Mammoth Theatre Company Experimental theater that puts on edgy and original works. (p111)

Studio Theatre Award-winning venue for contemporary plays, known for its powerhouse premieres. (p111)

Ford's Theatre Lincoln's assassination site is still an active playhouse, often staging works related to Abe. (p104; pictured)

Best Performing Arts

Kennedy Center DC's performing-arts king of the hill, home to the symphony, opera and more. (p67)

Busboys & Poets Nerve center for open-mic poetry readings and story slams. (p113)

Military Bands The Marine Corps, Air Force, Army and Navy make patriotic music at the Capitol.

National Theatre DC's glitzy grande dame hosts Broadway shows and big touring productions. (p111)

Best Comedy

DC Improv National stand-up comics yuck it up alongside local amateurs. (p125)

Top Tips

● Destination DC (www.washington.org/calendar) is good for event listings.

● Gold Star (www.goldstar.com/washington-dc) sells discounted tickets (up to 50% off) to local performances..

Art & Architecture

The National Gallery of Art and Reynolds Center for American Art & Portraiture are the big players, but Washington's art scene extends well beyond them. Specialty collections fill several smaller museums, and a host of galleries make their home in DC. The neoclassical, Federal-style and modern buildings are artworks in their own right.

ARCHITECT: DOUGLAS CARDINAL. IMAGE: ROB CRANDALL/SHUTTERSTOCK ©

Best Galleries

District of Columbia Arts Center Grassroots group shows thought-provoking emerging artists. (p131)

Touchstone Gallery Run by a group of 45 artists, Touchstone puts on vibrant contemporary exhibitions. (p105)

Dupont Underground Groovy exhibitions held in an abandoned streetcar station beneath Dupont Circle. (p117)

Best Lessor Museums

Textile Museum The nation's only collection of its kind, with galleries of splendid fabrics and carpets. (p64)

National Building Museum Exhibits on DC's architecture set in a dramatic, Corinthian-columned hall. (p104)

National Museum of Women in the Arts Works by Kahlo, O'Keeffe and 700 other female artists. (p105)

Best Modern Architecture

National Museum of the American Indian The curving limestone exterior blobs like an art-house amoeba. (pictured; p52)

National Gallery of Art IM Pei designed the angular, light-drenched east building. (p49)

Donald W Reynolds Center for American Art & Portraiture The courtyard's glass canopy is jaw-dropping. (p100)

Top Tip

○ Federal-style architecture was popular from around 1780 to 1830. It evoked the elegance of classical architecture with an emphasis on understatement. The best places to see it are Georgetown and Capitol Hill.

History & Politics

The president, Congress and the Supreme Court, the three pillars of US government, are here. In their orbit float the State Department, World Bank and embassies from around the globe. If you hadn't got the idea, power is why Washington exerts such a palpable buzz. There's a thrill in seeing all the history and politics up close.

010110010101101/SHUTTERSTOCK ©

Best Politico Bars

Off the Record Where Very Important People drink martinis, steps from the White House. (p66)

Round Robin Since 1850, bigwigs and lobbyists have swirled drinks and cut deals in this gilded bar. (p67)

Best Politico Restaurants

Le Diplomate DC's political glitterati flock here for a Parisian-style night out. (p107)

Old Ebbitt Grill Play spot-the-senator while cracking open an oyster. (p66)

Cafe Milano Famed place to twirl spaghetti and spy big shots in Georgetown. (p78)

Best for Seeing Politics in Action

Capitol Sit in on committee hearings to see how bills start winding their way toward becoming laws. (p82)

White House The protester-fueled political theater outside the building shows democracy at its finest. (p58)

Best Sites for History Buffs

Ford's Theatre View the box seat where President Lincoln was assassinated. (p104)

National Archives Ogle the Declaration of Independence on parchment under glass. (p98)

Lincoln Memorial Steps Stand where Martin Luther King Jr gave his 'I Have a Dream' speech. (p36)

Watergate Complex Check out the building synonymous with political scandal, thanks to Richard Nixon and his wiretaps. (p64)

Under the Radar

Washington DC has plenty of big ticket attractions for you to engage in, but don't leave the city without digging a litte deeper - there are a lot of alternative experiences to be had.

DANIEL M. SILVA/SHUTTERSTOCK ©

Alternative Neighborhoods

Brookland Known as 'Litte Rome' for the many churches and shrines in the neighborhood, Brookland hosts a creative scene of beer bars, stylish cafes, art studios and craft shops in Northeast DC. (Centered along 12th Street NE; M Red line to Brookland-CUA.)

Crowd-Free Museums

National Museum of African Art This Smithsonian museum is an oasis of calm amid the Mall's madness. Eye-popping masks, paintings, sculptures and beaded works brighten the subterranean galleries. (https://africa.si.edu/ 950 Independence Ave SW, DC 20560. 🕙 10am-5:30pm)

Tudor Place Formally owned by George Washington's step-granddaughter, the mansion features some of George's furnishings from Mount Vernon. (p76)

National Museum of Asian Art Another Mall museum that's often overlooked, this Smithsonian unit offers ancient ceramics and temple sculptures spread across two galleries. (p51)

Low-Key Monuments

Korean War Veterans Memorial The haunting tribute on the Mall (p34) depicts ghostly steel soldiers marching by a wall of etched faces.

African American Civil War Memorial Rifle-bearing troops who fought in the Union Army are immortalized in bronze near the U Street Metro station.

Wild Green Spaces

United States National Arboretum Learn your state tree amid 450 acres of meadowlands and wooded groves. (https://www.usna.usda.gov/ 3501 New York Avenue, NE; 🕙 8m-5pm; M Stadium Armory Station on the Blue and Orange lines)

Active DC

The nation's capital comes together in ways unexpected and touching when sports are at stake. It's the only thing that gets citizens as pumped as politics, and it's more accessible, if not quite as cutthroat. But residents don't just watch sports – they get active, too. Miles of trails cross the city, offering sweet hiking and cycling opportunities.

ROSTISLAV AGEEV/SHUTTERSTOCK ©

Best Spectator Sports

Nationals Park Cheap baseball tickets, the Racing Presidents, and hip eats make a fun evening. (p95)

Verizon Center The Capitals fight hard at hockey, and the Wizards shoot some mean hoops here. (p111)

Best Walking & Running

The Mall Nothing inspires a run like this big green lawn studded with monuments.

C&O Canal Towpath Bucolic trail a few steps from Georgetown's shopping frenzy. (p75)

Georgetown Waterfront Park Riverside path to watch yachts and take a break at outdoor cafes. (p73)

Dumbarton Oaks Park Escape the crowds on wooded, bridge-crossed trails. (p77)

Yards Park Amble the boardwalk along the Anacostia River. (p87)

Best Guided Jaunts

Key Bridge Boathouse Paddle by monuments on twilight kayaking tours. (p75)

Bike & Roll Nighttime cycling rides around the illuminated Mall. (p145)

Best Cycling

Big Wheel Bikes Convenient rental shop near three ace cycling trails. (p145)

Capital Bikeshare Stations around the city rent two-wheelers for quick trips. (p145)

Top Tip

○ For all spectator sports, buy tickets direct from the team's website or stadium box office, or via StubHub (www.stubhub.com).

Four Perfect Days

Day 1

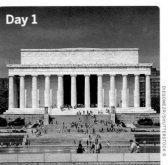

DEGOMEZR/SHUTTERSTOCK ©

Dive right into the good stuff. The **Lincoln Memorial,** (pictured; p36) is as iconically DC as it gets. Next up is the powerful **Vietnam Veterans Memorial** (p38). Then comes the **Washington Monument** (p40), DC's tallest structure.

Munch sandwiches by an artsy waterfall at **Cascade Cafe** (p53). After lunch, explore the **National Museum of African American History and Culture** (p48), assuming you've procured a ticket, or the **National Gallery of Art** (p49). Next, mosey across the lawn to the **National Air and Space Museum** (p42).

Hop on the Metro to Dupont Circle for dinner. Sip cocktails at **Bar Charley** (p123) or hoist brews with locals at **Board Room** (p117).

Day 2

ELISANK79/SHUTTERSTOCK ©

Go political this morning. Start in the **Capitol** (pictured; p82) and tour the statue-cluttered halls. Then walk up the grand steps to the **Supreme Court** (p90); The **Library of Congress** (p90) and its 500 miles of books blow minds next door.

Continue the government theme in the White House neighborhood. Have a burger amid politicos at **Old Ebbitt Grill** (p66). Did you book a **White House** (p58) tour? Zip over to the **Kennedy Center** (p67) for the free 6pm show.

Hit Georgetown for dinner. Maybe French fare at **Chez Billy Sud** (p78) or pizza at **Il Canale** (p77). Sink a pint in a friendly pub like the **Tombs** (p73). Outdoor cafes make **Georgetown Waterfront Park** (p73) a hot spot on warm nights.

Day 3

In **Arlington National Cemetery** (pictured; p138) you can't help but be moved by the 624 acres of memorials, tombs and of course JFK's eternal flame.

Spend the afternoon downtown and see the Declaration of Independence at the **National Archives** (p98), and the seat where Lincoln was shot at **Ford's Theatre** (p104). The **Reynolds Center for American Art & Portraiture** (p100) hangs sublime paintings. When hunger strikes, try **Rasika** (p107) or **Central Michel Richard** (p106).

Head up 14th St NW toward Logan Circle, a bountiful food and drink zone. Buzzy **Le Diplomate** (p107) wafts a Parisian vibe, while **Churchkey** (p108) pours 550 different beers.

Day 4

Start at Dupont Circle and walk NW on Massachusetts Ave gaping at **Embassy Row** (p120). The **Phillips Collection** (p120) spreads out in a Dupont manor; offering an hour or two of groovy modern art browsing.

Adams Morgan (pictured) sits north of Dupont. It's DC's party zone, but during the day **Meeps** (p135) and **Idle Time Books** (p135) provide plenty to do. Don't miss happy hour at **Songbyrd Record Cafe & Music House** (p134; pictured), a cool retro bar.

In the evening head to Columbia Heights and wander 11th St NW. In fine weather the patio benches at **Wonderland Ballroom** (p137) fill with locals enjoying libations. Try wine-pouring **Room 11** (p137), beer-and-pool bar **Meridian Pint** (p137).

Need to Know

For detailed information, see Survival Guide (p141)

Currency
US dollar ($)

Language
English

Visas
Nationals of 38 countries can enter the US without a visa but must fill out an ESTA application.

Money
ATMs ubiquitous. Credit cards widely accepted.

Cell Phones
International travelers can use local SIM cards in an unlocked phone (or else buy a cheap US phone and load it with prepaid minutes.)

Time
Eastern Standard Time (GMT/UTC minus five hours)

Tipping
Not optional. Restaurant servers 15%-20%. Bartenders 15% per round. Housekeeping staff $2 to $5 per night. Taxi drivers 10% to 15%.

Daily Budget

Budget: Less than $125
Dorm bed: $30–55
Lunchtime specials for food and happy-hour drinks: $15–30
Metro day pass: $14.50

Midrange: $125–350
Hotel or B&B double room: $150–275
Dinner in a casual restaurant: $15–25
Bicycle tour: $40

Top End: More than $350
Luxury hotel double room: $400
Dinner at Pineapple and Pearls: $280
Washington National Opera ticket: $100–200

Advance Planning

Three months Book your hotel, request a White House tour, try for tickets to the African American History and Culture Museum.

One month before Reserve tickets online for the National Archives, US Holocaust Memorial Museum, Ford's Theatre and Capitol tour.

Two weeks before Reserve ahead at your must-eat restaurants.

Arriving to Washington, DC

Washington Dulles International Airport is 26 miles west of DC. Ronald Reagan Washington National Airport is 4.5 miles south of downtown.

✈ From Ronald Reagan Washington National Airport

Metro trains (around $2.60) depart every 10 minutes between 5am and midnight (to 3am Friday and Saturday) for the 20 minute journey. A taxi is $15 to $22.

✈ From Washington Dulles International Airport

The Silver Line Express bus runs every 15 minutes from Dulles to Wiehle-Reston East Metro between 6am and 10:40pm (from 7:45am weekends). Time to the city center is 75 minutes; tickets around $11. A taxi is $62 to $73.

🚇 From Union Station

All trains and many buses arrive here (pictured below). There's a Metro stop inside for easy onward transport.

Getting Around

The public-transportation system is a mix of Metro trains and buses. Buy a rechargeable SmarTrip card at any Metro station.

Ⓜ Metro

DC's subway system runs from 5am to midnight (3am on weekends). Fares from $1.85 to $6. A day pass costs $14.50.

🚌 Bus

Red DC Circulator buses are useful for areas with limited Metro service. Fare is $1.

🚕 Taxi

Taxis are relatively easy to find, but costly. Fares are $2.16 per mile; the meter starts at $3.25.

Washington, DC Neighborhoods

Dupont Circle (p115)
A well-heeled splice of gay community and DC diplomatic scene. Dupont boasts stylish restaurants, cocktail bars and cozy cafes.

Georgetown (p71)
University students, academics and senators call this aristocratic area home. Chichi shops and winsome cafes line the streets.

Whitehouse Area & Foggy Bottom (p57)
The President's 'hood hums with federal business by day and performing arts by night.

White House

Vietnam Veterans Memorial

Washingto Monumen

Lincoln Memorial

US Holocaust Memorial Museum

Arlington National Cemetery

National Mall (p35)
This big green space holds most of the major museums and monuments.

Adams Morgan (p129)
Browse vintage boutiques by day, dive into bars and clubs by night. Eat well at romantic bistros and ethnic joints anytime.

Downtown Penn Quarter & Logan Circle (p97)
It's a museum mecca, theatre district and convention hub peppered with snazzy eateries.

Reynolds Center for American Art & Portraiture ◉
◉ National Archives
◉ Capitol
◉
National Air & Space Museum

Capitol Hill (p81)
Home to the Capitol, Supreme Court and other landmarks, it's also a hub of markets, homey restaurants and cheery bars.

Worth a Trip (p138)
Arlington National Cemetary

Explore
Washington, DC

National Mall **35**

**White House Area
and Foggy Bottom** **57**

Georgetown 71

Capitol Hill **81**

**Downtown, Penn Quarter
& Logan Circle** **97**

Dupont Circle 115

Adams Morgan **129**

Washington, DC's Walking Tours 🥾

Iconic Washington 54

Strolling Genteel Georgetown 72

A Capital Day on Capitol Hill 86

Exploring Jazzy U Street & Shaw 112

A Night out in Dupont Circle 116

Embassies & Mansions 126

Mixing it up in Columbia Heights 136

The Reflecting Pool in front of the Lincoln Memorial (p36)
010110010101101/SHUTTERSTOCK ©

Explore ⊚
The National Mall

Folks often call the Mall 'America's Front Yard.' It is indeed a lawn, unfurling two miles of scrubby green grass from the Capitol west to the Lincoln Memorial. It's also where citizens come to protest their government, and connect with the nation's most-cherished ideals writ large in monuments and museums.

The Short List

○ **Lincoln Memorial (p36)** *Staring into Abe's stony eyes, reading his Gettysburg Address and standing where Martin Luther King Jr gave his 'I Have a Dream' speech.*

○ **National Museum of African American History and Culture (p48)** *Learning about the diverse African American experience and how it shapes the nation.*

○ **National Air and Space Museum (p42)** *Marveling at the technological innovation in the craft that have transported humans into the sky and space.*

○ **National Gallery of Art (p49)** *Gazing at hundreds of masterpieces in two cleverly connected buildings.*

○ **Vietnam Veterans Memorial (p38)** *Reflecting on the sea of names etched into this evocative memorial.*

Getting There & Around

Ⓜ Smithsonian (Orange, Silver, Blue Lines) and L'Enfant Plaza (Orange, Silver, Blue, Green and Yellow Lines) for most sights; Foggy Bottom-GWU (Orange, Silver, Blue Lines) for the Lincoln and Vietnam Memorials – though they're about a mile walk from the station.

🚌 The DC Circulator National Mall bus goes from Union Station around the Mall and Tidal Basin, with stops at main sights.

Neighborhood Map on p46

The Washington Monument (p40) KEN SCHULZE/SHUTTERSTOCK ©

Top Experience 📷
Admire the Lincoln Memorial

In a city of icons, the monument for the nation's 16th president stands out in the crowd. Maybe it's the classicism evoked by the Greek temple design, or the stony dignity of Lincoln's gaze. Whatever the lure, a visit here while looking out over the Reflecting Pool is a defining DC moment.

◎ MAP P46, A4

📞 202-426-6841

www.nps.gov/linc

2 Lincoln Memorial Circle NW

🕐 24hr

The Columns

Plans for a monument to Abraham Lincoln began in 1867 – two years after his assassination – but construction didn't begin until 1914. Henry Bacon designed the memorial to resemble a Doric temple, with 36 columns to represent the 36 states in Lincoln's union.

The Statue & Words

Carvers used 28 blocks of marble to fashion the seated figure. Lincoln's face and hands are particularly realistic, since they are based on castings done when he was president. The words of his Gettysburg Address and Second Inaugural speech flank the statue on the north and south walls, along with murals depicting his principles. Look for symbolic images of freedom, liberty and unity, among others.

MLK Marker

From the get-go, the Lincoln Memorial became a symbol of the Civil Rights movement. Most famously, Martin Luther King Jr gave his 'I Have a Dream' speech here in 1963. An engraving of King's words marks the spot where he stood. It's on the landing, 18 steps from the top, and is usually where everyone is gathered, snapping photos of the awesome view out over the Mall.

Reflecting Pool

Architect Henry Bacon also conceived the iconic Reflecting Pool, modeling it on the canals at Versailles and Fontainebleau. The 0.3-mile-long pond holds 6.75 million gallons of water that circulate in from the nearby Tidal Basin.

★ Top Tips

o Visit the memorial at night. It's well lit and particularly atmospheric once the sun sets (plus there's less crowd jostling).

o For a dramatic view of the Reflecting Pool and Washington Monument, stand on Martin Luther King Jr's step.

o A small exhibit hall lies under the memorial to the south side of the steps. A larger space is being developed as part of a $25 million refurbishment of the memorial.

✕ Take a Break

For coffee, craft cocktails, beer and wine, hit the casual little bar in **Hotel Hive** (☎202-849-8499; www.hotelhive.com; 2224 F St NW, Foggy Bottom; d $150, loft r $149-229; ❄ 🛜 🐾; Ⓜ Orange, Silver, Blue Line to Foggy Bottom-GWU). It also houses an outpost of a local pizza chain that's open from morning until late. It's 0.75 miles north of the memorial on 23rd St NW in the Foggy Bottom area.

Top Experience 📷

Reflect & Remember at the Vietnam Veterans Memorial

A black granite 'V' cuts into the Mall, just as the war it memorializes cut into the national psyche. The monument eschews mixing conflict with glory. Instead, it quietly records the names of service personnel killed or missing in action in Vietnam, honoring those who gave their lives and explaining, in stark architectural language, the true price paid in war.

◉ MAP P46, A3

www.nps.gov/vive

5 Henry Bacon Dr NW

🕙 24hr

🚌 Circulator National Mall, Ⓜ Orange, Silver, Blue Line to Foggy Bottom-GWU

The Design

Maya Lin, a 21-year-old Yale architecture student, designed the memorial following a nationwide competition in 1981. The 'V' is comprised of two walls of polished granite that meet in the center at a 10ft peak, then taper to a height of 8in. The mirror-like surface lets visitors see their own reflection among the names of the dead, bringing past and present together.

Order of Names

The wall lists soldiers' names chronologically according to the date they died (and alphabetically within each day). The list starts at the monument's vertex on panel 1E on July 8, 1959. It moves day by day to the end of the eastern wall at panel 70E, then starts again at panel 70W at the western wall's end. It returns to the vertex on May 15, 1975, where the war's beginning and end meet in symbolic closure.

Mementos, Diamonds & Plus Signs

A diamond next to the name indicates 'killed, body recovered.' A plus sign indicates 'missing and unaccounted for.' There are approximately 1200 of the latter. If a soldier returns alive, a circle is inscribed around the plus sign. To date, no circles appear.

Reaction & Nearby Sculptures

In 1984, vocal critics of Maya Lin's design insisted that a more traditional sculpture be added to the monument. Frederick Hart's bronze Three Servicemen statue depicts three soldiers – one white, one African American and one Latino – who seem to be gazing upon the nearby sea of names. The tree-ringed Vietnam Women's Memorial, showing female soldiers aiding a fallen combatant, is also nearby.

★ Top Tips

o Paper indices at each end of the wall let you look up individual names and get their panel location. Or you can look electronically via the Vietnam Veterans Memorial Fund (www.vvmf.org/Wall-of-Faces), which also provides photos and further info on each name.

o If you have questions, national park rangers are on-site from 10am to 10pm.

✕ Take a Break

Food trucks congregate on Constitution Ave, behind the National Museum of African American History and Culture.

The two bars and restaurant in the fashionable Watergate Hotel (p64) are only a 0.8 mile walk away.

Top Experience 📷
Enjoy Sweeping Views from the Washington Monument

Rising on the Mall like an exclamation point, this 555ft obelisk embodies the awe and respect the nation felt for George Washington, the USA's first president and founding father. The monument is DC's loftiest structure, and by federal law no local building can reach above it.

◎ MAP P46, D4

www.nps.gov/wamo

2 15th St NW

admission free

🚋 Circulator National Mall, Ⓜ Orange, Silver, Blue Line to Smithsonian

Mismatched Marble

Construction began in 1848, but a lack of funds during the Civil War grounded the monument at 156ft. By the time work began again in 1876, the quarry that had provided the original marble had dried up. Contractors had to go elsewhere for the rest of the rock. Look closely for the delineation in color where the old and new marble meet about a third of the way up (the bottom is a bit lighter).

Pyramid Topper

In December 1884, workers heaved a 3300lb marble capstone onto the monument and topped it off with a 9in pyramid of cast aluminum. At the time, aluminum was rare and expensive. Before the shiny novelty went to Washington, the designers displayed the pyramid in the window of Tiffany's in New York City.

Observation Deck & Memorial Stones

Inside the monument, an elevator takes you to the sky-high observation deck that provides grand city vistas. On the way back down, the elevator slows so you can glimpse some of the 195 memorial stones that decorate the shaft's interior.

Lines & Tickets

You'll need a ticket to get in. Same-day passes for a timed entrance are available at the **kiosk** (15th St, btwn Madison Dr NW & Jefferson Dr SW; 🚃 Circulator National Mall, Ⓜ Orange, Silver, Blue Lines to Smithsonian) by the monument. During peak season reserve tickets in advance by phone (877-444-6777) or online (www.recreation.gov) for a small fee.

★ Top Tips

○ Arrive 10 minutes before your ticket time, since you'll have to go through security first. The entrance area is small, and only a handful of people can enter at once.

○ Allow an hour for your visit from start to finish. You're welcome to stay longer – no one pushes you out – but an hour is the average most people spend.

○ Don't bring food, drinks or large backpacks. You're not allowed to take them up to the observation deck, and there are no storage lockers to put them in at the entrance.

✗ Take a Break

Eat a sandwich beside avant-garde sculptures at the Pavilion Cafe (p53).

Grab a gelato at **Dolcezza at Hirshhorn** (www.dolcezzagelato.com; Hirshhorn Museum, cnr 7th St & Independence Ave SW; gelato $4, pastries $2-7; ⊙ 9am-5pm Mon-Fri, 10am Sat & Sun; 🛜

Top Experience 📷

Let Your Mind Take Flight at the National Air and Space Museum

The Air and Space Museum is among the Smithsonian's biggest crowd-pullers. Families flock here to view the mind-blowing array of planes, rockets and other contraptions – and all of it is as rousing for adults as kids. Name the historic aircraft or spacecraft – the Wright Brothers' flyer, Lindbergh's Spirit of St Louis, Skylab – and it's bound to be on one of the museum's two chock-a-block floors.

◉ MAP P46, G4

www.airandspace.si.edu

6th St & Independence Ave

🕙 10am-5:30pm

🚌 Circulator National Mall,
Ⓜ Orange, Silver, Blue,
Green Line to L'Enfant Plaza

Milestones of Flight Hall

The museum's entrance hall makes an impression. Walk in the Mall-side entrance and look up: Chuck Yeager's sound-barrier-breaking Bell X-1 and Charles Lindbergh's transatlantic-crossing *Spirit of St Louis* hang from the ceiling. Nuclear missiles rise up from the floor.

1903 Wright Flyer

The Wright Brothers get their own gallery (2nd floor), and its centerpiece is the 1903 biplane they built and flew at Kitty Hawk, North Carolina in 1903. That's right: the world's first airplane is here. Also on display is a bicycle the brothers designed.

Amelia Earhart's Plane

Amelia Earhart's natty red Lockheed 5B Vega shines in the Pioneers of Flight gallery (2nd floor). She dubbed it her 'Little Red Bus' and in 1932 flew it solo across the Atlantic Ocean – a first for a woman. A few months later she flew it nonstop across the US, a 19-hour journey from Los Angeles to Newark, NJ, another female first.

Apollo Lunar Module

It looks like it's made of tinfoil, but the Apollo Lunar Module was designed to carry astronauts to the moon. The unit on display was only used for ground testing, and was subsequently modified to resemble the module that Neil Armstrong and Buzz Aldrin stepped out of as the first men on the moon.

Skylab Orbital Workshop

Skylab was America's first space station, launched in 1973. The orbital workshop was its largest component, and was where the astronauts lived. Crews of three stayed aboard for up to three months. Walk through to see the shower, exercise bicycle and other cramped quarters.

★ Top Tips

o Stop by the information desk and pick up a map, which shows where all the highlights are located.

o Download the museum's free GO FLIGHT app, either before you arrive or on-site using the free wi-fi. It provides extra content about popular items in the collection.

o Free 90-minute tours depart from the welcome center daily at 10:30am and 1pm. More tours are often added if guides are available.

✕ Take a Break

The foyer cafe at the neighboring Hirshhorn Museum (p41) serves coffee, pastries and delectable handmade gelato.

For something more substantial, try the Mitsitam Native Foods Cafe (p52) in the adjacent American Indian Museum.

How Things Fly Gallery

On the 1st floor near the welcome center, How Things Fly whooshes with interactive gadgets. Kids can find out their weight on the moon, see a wind tunnel in action and make awesome paper airplanes.

Flight Simulators

Thrill-seekers should head to the Flight Simulator Zone on the 1st floor. You can take a badass VR Transporter experience where you will fly a combat sortie in a simulator that lets you control the action and perform 360-degree barrel rolls.

Imax Theater & Planetarium

The Lockheed Martin Imax Theater screens films throughout the day.

Shows at the Albert Einstein Planetarium send viewers hurtling through space. Buy your tickets as soon as you arrive, or on the museum website before you visit. ($9 for adults, $7.50 for children).

Museum Annex

Only a fraction of the museum's planes and spacecraft fit into the building on the Mall. The leftovers fill two enormous hangars at the Steven F Udvar-Hazy Center near Dulles Airport (pictured below). Highlights include the *Enola Gay* (the B-29 that dropped the atomic bomb on Hiroshima) and Space Shuttle *Discovery*. The annex is 2½ miles (about a $12 taxi ride) from Dulles.

Who Was James Smithson?

The Big Gift

James Smithson was a British scientist who never set foot in the USA, let alone Washington, DC. Yet he died in 1829 with a provision in his will to found 'at Washington, under the name of the Smithsonian Institution, an establishment for the increase and diffusion of knowledge.' Actually, that was the backup plan. The money first went to his nephew Henry, but Henry died a few years after Smithson, without heirs. So the 'institution' clause kicked in, and $508,318 arrived in Washington for the task.

The US government promptly ignored the amazing gift. Various senators grumbled it was undignified for America to accept such presents, particularly from an unknown foreigner. Anti-British sentiment informed some of this debate: the 1814 British torching of Washington remained fresh in many American minds. Finally though, Congress accepted the money and began constructing the Smithsonian Institution in 1846.

Mysterious Motive

So who was Smithson? A mineralogist by trade and shrewd investor by evidence, Smithson was well educated and wealthy. But his motivations for bequeathing so much money to the USA, as opposed to his native Britain, remain a mystery. Some say he was an anti-monarchist who took a particular shine to the American Republic. He may have just loved learning.

Smithson was 64 when he died in Genoa, Italy, and was buried there, until Alexander Graham Bell – in his role as Smithsonian regent – went to fetch the Englishman's remains and bring them to Washington in 1904. Today Smithson is entombed in the Smithsonian Castle on the Mall.

The Smithsonian Today

Smithson's gift morphed into a vast vault of treasures. The Smithsonian holds approximately 156 million artworks, scientific specimens, artifacts and other objects, of which less than 2% are on display at any given time.

The collection sprawls across 19 museums – 10 on the Mall, seven others around DC and two in New York City. The Smithsonian also operates the National Zoo. There is no entry fee for any of the venues. They're all free, always.

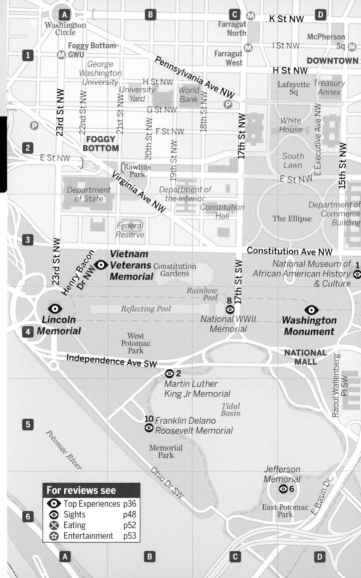

The National Mall

For reviews see

◉ Top Experiences	p36
◉ Sights	p48
✕ Eating	p52
★ Entertainment	p53

The National Mall

Sights

National Museum of African American History & Culture

MUSEUM

1 MAP P46, D3

This sensational museum covers the diverse African American experience and how it helped shape the nation. Start downstairs in the sobering 'Slavery and Freedom' exhibition and work your way up to the community and culture galleries on the 3rd and 4th floors, where African American achievements in sport, music, theater and visual arts are joyfully celebrated. Artifacts, state-of-the-art interactive exhibits, site-specific artworks and fascinating interpretative panels abound in the cleverly designed exhibition spaces. (☎844-750-3012; www.nmaahc.si.edu; 1400 Constitution Ave NW; admission free; ⏰10am-5:30pm; 🚶; 🚌Circulator National Mall, ⓂOrange, Silver, Blue Line to Smithsonian or Federal Triangle)

Martin Luther King Jr Memorial

MONUMENT

2 MAP P46, B4

Opened in 2011, this was the first Mall memorial to honor an African American. Sculptor Lei Yixin carved the piece, which is reminiscent in concept and style to the Mt Rushmore memorial. Besides Dr King's striking, 30ft-tall image, known as the Stone of Hope, there are two blocks of granite behind him that represent the Mountain of Despair. A wall inscribed with

The National Gallery of Art

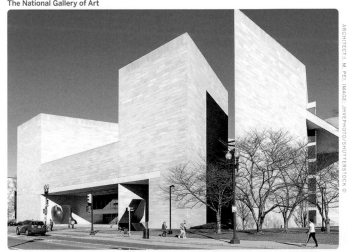

King's powerful quotes about democracy, justice and peace flank the piece. (www.nps.gov/mlkm; 1964 Independence Ave SW; ⏱24hr; 🚊Circulator National Mall, Ⓜ Orange, Silver, Blue Line to Smithsonian)

National Gallery of Art MUSEUM

3 ◎ MAP P46, G3

Two buildings. Hundreds of masterpieces. Infinite enjoyment. The neoclassical **West Building** showcases European art through to the early 1900s; highlights include works by da Vinci, Manet, Monet and Van Gogh. The IM Pei–designed **East Building** displays modern and contemporary art – don't miss Pollock's *Number 1, 1950 (Lavender Mist),* Picasso's *Family of Saltimbanques* and the massive Calder mobile specially commissioned for the entrance lobby. An underground walkway connects the buildings and is made extraordinary by Leo Villareal's light sculpture, *Multiverse.* (📞202-737-4215; www.nga.gov; Constitution Ave NW, btwn 3rd & 7th Sts; admission free; ⏱10am-5pm Mon-Sat, 11am-6pm Sun; ♿; 🚊Circulator National Mall, Ⓜ Green, Yellow Line to Archives-Navy Memorial-Penn Quarter)

National Museum of American History MUSEUM

4 ◎ MAP P46, E3

Containing all kinds of artifacts of the American experience, this museum has as its centerpiece the flag that flew over Baltimore's Fort McHenry during the War of 1812 – the same flag that inspired Francis Scott Key to pen 'The Star-Spangled Banner' (it's on the entry level). Other highlights include Julia Child's kitchen (1st floor) and 'The First Ladies' costume exhibit on the 3rd floor. New exhibits include 'American Enterprise' (1st floor) and 'On with the Show' (3rd floor). (📞202-633-1000; www.americanhistory.si.edu; 1300 Constitution Ave NW, btwn 12th and 14th Sts NW; admission free; ⏱10am-5:30pm, to 7:30pm some days; ♿; 🚊Circulator National Mall, Ⓜ Orange, Silver, Blue Line to Smithsonian or Federal Triangle)

National Museum of Natural History MUSEUM

5 ◎ MAP P46, F3

Arguably the most popular of the Smithsonian museums, so crowds are pretty much guaranteed. Wave to Henry, the elephant who guards the rotunda, then zip to the 2nd floor's Hope Diamond, a 45.52-karat bauble that's said to have cursed its owners, which included Marie Antoinette. The giant squid (1st floor, Ocean Hall), live butterfly pavilion and tarantula feedings provide additional thrills at this kid-packed venue. The beloved dinosaur hall, centered on the Nation's T-Rex, has reopened after being revamped. (📞202-663-1000; www.naturalhistory.si.edu; cnr 10th St & Constitution Ave NW; admission free; ⏱10am-5:30pm, to 7:30pm some days; ♿; 🚊Circulator National Mall, Ⓜ Orange, Silver, Blue Line to Smithsonian or Federal Triangle)

Mall of Justice

The Mall has long provided a forum for people seeking to make their grievances heard by the government. Suffragists, veterans, peaceniks, civil-rights activists, sharecroppers and million-mom marchers, among many other groups, have all staged political rallies on the Mall over the years.

Key Events in History

o **Bonus Army** (1932) WWI veterans, left unemployed by the Great Depression, petitioned the government for an early payment of promised bonuses for their wartime service. As many as 10,000 veterans settled in for an extended protest, pitching tents on the Mall and the Capitol lawn.

o **'I Have a Dream'** (1963) At the zenith of the Civil Rights movement, Reverend Martin Luther King's stirring speech, delivered from the steps of the Lincoln Memorial to 200,000 supporters, remains a high point in the struggle for racial equality.

o **Anti-War Protests** (1971) In April 1971 an estimated 500,000 Vietnam veterans and students gathered on the Mall to oppose continued hostilities. Several thousand arrests were made.

o **AIDS Memorial Quilt** (1996) Gay and lesbian activists drew more than 300,000 supporters in a show of solidarity for equal rights under the law and to display the ever-growing AIDS quilt, which covered the entire eastern flank of the Mall from the Capitol to the Washington Monument.

o **Million-Mom March** (2000) A half-million people convened on the Mall on Mother's Day to draw attention to handgun violence and to demand that Congress pass stricter gun-ownership laws.

o **Bring Them Home Now Tour** (2005) Led by families who lost loved ones in the war, this gathering of over 100,000 protesters demanded the withdrawal of American soldiers from Iraq.

o **Women's March** (2017) The day after President Donald Trump's inauguration, some 500,000 people gathered on the Mall to advocate for women's rights and other issues. Concurrent marches were held in cities around the globe.

Jefferson Memorial MONUMENT

6 MAP P46, D6

Set on the south bank of the Tidal Basin amid the cherry trees, this memorial honors the third US president, political philosopher, drafter of the Declaration of Independence and founder of the University of Virginia. Designed by John Russell Pope in the style of the ancient Roman Pantheon, the rounded, open-air monument was initially derided by critics as 'the Jefferson Muffin.' Inside is a 19ft bronze likeness, and excerpts from Jefferson's writings are etched into the walls. (☏202-426-6841; www.nps.gov/thje; 13 E Basin Dr SW; ⊙24hr; ⬚Circulator National Mall, ⓂOrange, Silver, Blue Line to Smithsonian)

National Museum of Asian Art MUSEUM

7 MAP P46, E4

This is a lovely spot in which to while away a Washington afternoon. Japanese silk scrolls, smiling Buddhas, rare Islamic manuscripts and Chinese jades are exhibited in cool, quiet galleries in two museums connected by an underground tunnel. The Freer section also houses works by American painter James Whistler, including five *Nocturnes*. Don't miss the extraordinarily beautiful blue-and-gold Peacock Room on its ground floor, designed by Whistler in 1876–77 as an exotic showcase for a shipping magnate's Chinese porcelain collection. (☏202-633-1000; www.

National Sculpture Garden

The six-acre **National Sculpture Garden** at the **National Gallery of Art** (p49) is studded with whimsical sculptures such as Roy Lichtenstein's *House* and Louise Bourgeois' leggy *Spider*. They are scattered around a fountain – a great place to dip your feet in summer. From mid-November to mid-March the fountain becomes a festive ice rink.

asia.si.edu; 1050 Independence Ave SW; admission free; ⊙10am-5:30pm; ⬚Circulator National Mall, ⓂOrange, Silver, Blue Line to Smithsonian)

National WWII Memorial MONUMENT

8 MAP P46, C4

Dedicated in 2004, this grandiose memorial honors the 16 million US soldiers who served in WWII. Groups of veterans regularly come here to pay their respects to the 400,000 Americans who died as a result of the conflict. The plaza's dual arches symbolize victory in the Atlantic and Pacific theaters, and the 56 surrounding pillars represent each US state and territory. (www.nps.gov/wwii; 17th St SW; ⊙24hr; ⬚Circulator National Mall, ⓂOrange, Silver, Blue Line to Smithsonian)

National Museum of the American Indian

MUSEUM

9 ◎ MAP P46, H4

Ensconced in an architecturally notable building, this museum offers cultural artifacts related to the indigenous people of the Americas. Sadly, navigation of the exhibits is confusing on both a curatorial and physical level. The 'Our Universes' gallery (on the 4th floor) about Native American beliefs and creation stories is one of the more interesting exhibits. (📞202-633-1000; www. americanindian.si.edu; cnr 4th St & Independence Ave SW; admission free; ⏰10am-5:30pm; 👬; 🚌Circulator National Mall, Ⓜ Orange, Silver, Blue, Green, Yellow Line to L'Enfant Plaza)

Franklin Delano Roosevelt Memorial

MONUMENT

10 ◎ MAP P46, B5

The 7.5-acre memorial pays tribute to the longest-serving president in US history. Visitors are taken through four red-granite areas

that narrate FDR's time in office, from the Depression to the New Deal to WWII. The story is told through statuary and inscriptions, punctuated with fountains and peaceful alcoves. It's especially pretty at night. The irony is that FDR didn't want a grand memorial. Instead, he requested a modest **stone slab** (cnr 9th St & Pennsylvania Ave NW, Penn Quarter; Ⓜ Green, Yellow Line to Archives) by the Archives building. DC honored that request too. (www.nps.gov/frde; 400 W Basin Dr SW; ⏰24hr; 🚌Circulator National Mall, Ⓜ Orange, Silver, Blue Line to Smithsonian)

Eating

Mitsitam Native Foods Cafe

NATIVE AMERICAN $$

Certainly the most unique food on the Mall, Mitsitam (see **9** ◎ Map p46, H4) introduces visitors to the Native American cuisine of five different regions, including the Northwest coast (think cedar-planked wild salmon), Great Plains (buffalo chili) and northern woodlands (maple-brined turkey and wild rice). There are also fast-food staples including tacos, *totopos* (corn tortilla chips) and buffalo and elk burgers. It's a cafeteria-style setup. (www.mitsitamcafe.com; cnr 4th St & Independence Ave SW, National Museum of the American Indian; mains $12-22; ⏰11am-5pm late May-early Sep, to 3pm rest of year; 🚌Circulator National Mall, Ⓜ Orange, Silver, Blue, Green, Yellow Line to L'Enfant Plaza)

Bring a Picnic

Aside from a couple of museum cafes and scattered snack vendors, it's a food desert on the Mall. It's wise to bring your own nibbles. One strategy: hit Eastern Market first to assemble a picnic for later. It's a short hop east on the Metro's Blue, Orange and Silver Lines in the Capitol Hill neighborhood.

Pavilion Cafe

CAFE $

11 ❽ MAP P46, F3

A pocket of Paris secreted on the edge of the National Gallery of Art's Sculpture Garden, this cafeteria is housed in a glass pavilion whose design was inspired by the metro signs designed by art nouveau master, Hector Guimard. Head here to enjoy a salad, sandwich or pastry accompanied by tea, coffee or wine. (📞202-289-3361; www.pavilioncafe.com; cnr Constitution Ave & 7th St NW, National Gallery of Art Sculpture Garden; sandwiches $10-12, salads $11-13; ⏲10am-4pm Mon-Sat, 11am-5pm Sun, seasonal late openings; 🚌Circulator National Mall, Ⓜ Green, Yellow Line to Archives-Navy Memorial-Penn Quarter)

Cascade Café

CAFE $

12 ❽ MAP P46, H3

Located at the juncture of the National Gallery's two wings, the Cascade offers views of just that: a shimmering, IM Pei-designed artificial waterfall. The cafeteria-style restaurant is divided into different stations where you pick up a tray and choose from pizza, pasta, sandwiches, barbecue and salads. An espresso bar serves coffee, pastries and gelato. (📞202-842-6679; www.nga.gov/visit/cafes/cascade-cafe.html; National Gallery of Art, Constitution Ave NW, East Bldg, concourse; sandwiches $7-9.50; ⏲11am-3pm Mon-Sat, to 4pm Sun; 🚻; 🚌Circulator National Mall, Ⓜ Green, Yellow Line to Archives-Navy Memorial-Penn Quarter)

Entertainment

Jazz in the Garden

LIVE MUSIC

13 ⭐ MAP P46, F3

Lots of locals show up for these free outdoor jazz, blues and world-music concerts at the **National Gallery of Art Sculpture Garden** (www.nga.gov; cnr Constitution Ave NW & 7th St NW; admission free; ⏲10am-7pm Mon-Thu & Sat, to 9:30pm Fri, 11am-7pm Sun late May-early Oct, 10am-5pm Mon-Sat, 11am-6pm Sun early Oct-late May; 🚻; 🚌Circulator National Mall, Ⓜ Green, Yellow Line to Archives-Navy Memorial-Penn Quarter). Bring a blanket and picnic food, and supplement with beverages from the on-site Pavilion Cafe (p53). (📞202-842-6941; www.nga.gov/jazz; cnr Constitution Ave & 7th St NW; admission free; ⏲5-8:30pm Fri late May-late Aug; 🚌Circulator, Ⓜ Green, Yellow Line to Archives)

Discovery Theater

THEATER

14 ⭐ MAP P46, F4

In the basement of the Ripley Center, the Smithsonian's Discovery stages delightful puppet shows and other live educational performances for children aged two to 11 years. (📞202-633-8700; www.discoverytheater.org; 1100 Jefferson Dr SW, Ripley Center; tickets $6; 🚻; 🚌Circulator, Ⓜ Orange, Silver, Blue Line to Smithsonian)

Walking Tour 🥾

Iconic Washington

This is a hit parade of DC's most celebrated sights. They huddle around the National Mall – 'America's front yard' – the 2-mile-long strip of grass between the Capitol and Lincoln Memorial. Iconic monuments dot the grounds to the west, hulking Smithsonian museums to the east, and at the northern edge the White House. Start early, especially in summer, to avoid the crowds and the heat.

Start Vietnam Veterans Memorial; National Mall Circulator; Foggy Bottom-GWU

Finish White House; Federal Triangle or McPherson Sq

Length 3.75 miles; 2½ hours

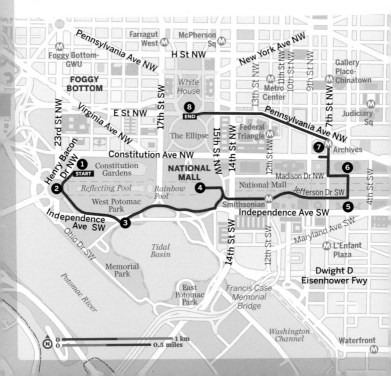

❶ Vietnam Veterans Memorial

The **Vietnam Veterans Memorial** (p38) reflects a roll call of the war's 53,000-plus American casualties. Check the symbol beside each name. A diamond indicates 'killed, body recovered.' A plus sign indicates 'missing and unaccounted for.' There are approximately 1200 of the latter.

❷ Lincoln Memorial

Follow the masses to the **Lincoln Memorial** (p36). Commune with Abe in his chair, then head down the steps to the marker where Martin Luther King Jr gave his 'Dream' speech. From here, the view of the Reflecting Pool and Washington Monument is one of DC's best.

❸ Martin Luther King Jr Memorial

Mosey to the Tidal Basin; the **Martin Luther King Jr Memorial** (p48) stands by the water. Walk right around the towering statue and read the quotes on the walls.

❹ Washington Monument

As you approach the **Washington Monument** (p40) look a third of the way up. See how it's slightly lighter in color at the bottom?

Builders had to use different marble after the first source dried up.

❺ National Air & Space Museum

Simply step inside the **Air & Space Museum** (p42) and gaze up. Lindbergh's *Spirit of St Louis* and Chuck Yeager's sound-barrier breaking *Bell X-1* are among the history-making machines that hang from the ceiling.

❻ National Gallery of Art

Walk across the Mall to the neoclassical west building of the **National Gallery of Art** (p49). Ogle the Western Hemisphere's only Leonardo da Vinci painting in Gallery 6. The east building hangs works by Picasso, Matisse and other modern masters.

❼ National Archives

Enter the rotunda at the **National Archives** (p98). The Declaration of Independence, Constitution and Bill of Rights unfurl on parchment under glass.

❽ White House

Stroll up Pennsylvania Ave to E St NW and the **White House** (p58). Snap pictures across the South Lawn. Bonus points if you capture a helicopter landing on the grass.

Explore

White House Area & Foggy Bottom

The president lives at the center of the 'hood. The State Department, World Bank and other institutions hover nearby in Foggy Bottom. A business district by day and not terribly active by night.

The Short List

o **White House (p58)** *Wandering ornately decorated reception rooms, viewing portraits of presidents and their wives, and perhaps bumping into Lincoln's ghost roaming the halls at the president's official abode.*

o **Round Robin (p67)** *Knocking back a Scotch or mint julep at one of the US's most famous hotel bars.*

o **Kennedy Center (p67)** *Watching a free performance any night of the week at this massive cultural center on the banks of the Potomac River.*

o **Textile Museum (p64)** *Browsing exhibitions of exquisite fabrics and weavings from across the globe.*

o **Old Ebbitt Grill (p66)** *Playing spot-the-politician while slurping oysters and sipping cocktails at this boisterous tavern near the White House.*

Getting There & Around

Ⓜ The Orange, Silver and Blue Lines run in tandem here. Get off at Federal Triangle or McPherson Sq for the White House; Farragut West for the Renwick and other museums; and Foggy Bottom-GWU for the university and Kennedy Center.

🚌 A free shuttle runs every 15 minutes between the Foggy Bottom-GWU Metro station and the Kennedy Center.

Neighborhood Map on p62

The Old Ebbitt Grill (p66). ROBERT ALEXANDER/GETTY IMAGES ©

Top Experience 📷

Visit the President at the White House

The White House is a home as well as a symbol. It stuns visitors with its sense of pomp and circumstance, yet it also charms with little traces left behind by those who have lived here before, which includes every US president since John Adams. Icon of the American presidency? Yeah. But it's also someone's home.

◉ MAP P62, F4

www.whitehouse.gov

1600 Pennsylvania Ave NW, White House Area

🕑 tours 7:30-11:30am Tue-Thu, to 1:30pm Fri & Sat

Ⓜ Orange, Silver, Blue Line to Federal Triangle or McPherson Sq

The Design

George Washington picked the site for the White House in 1791. Pierre L'Enfant was the initial architect, but he was fired for insubordination. Washington held a national competition to find a new designer. Irish-born architect James Hoban won. Hoban's idea was to make the building simple and conservative, so as not to seem royal, in keeping with the new country's principles. He modeled the neoclassical-style manor on Leinster House, a mid-18th-century duke's villa in Dublin that still stands and is now used by Ireland's Parliament.

The Color

The 'President's House' was built between 1792 and 1800. Legend has it that after the British burned the building in the War of 1812, the house was restored and painted white to cover the smoke marks, and people began to call it the White House. That's not true – it had been white almost from the get-go – but it makes a nice story. Hoban, incidentally, was hired to supervise the rebuilding. It was a big job, as all that remained were the exterior walls and interior brickwork.

The Residence

The White House has 132 rooms and 35 bathrooms. This includes 412 doors, 147 windows, 28 fireplaces, eight staircases and three elevators (for those who are counting). The Residence is in the middle, flanked by the East and West Wings. The Residence has three main levels: the Ground Floor, State Floor and Second Floor. The Ground and State Floors have rooms used for official entertaining and ceremonial functions (many of which you see on the tour). The Second Floor holds the private living quarters of the president and family.

★ Top Tips

∘ Bring your smartphone or compact camera. Photos are permitted on the tours using these devices, though no video, flash photography or lenses longer than 3in are allowed.

∘ Do not bring backpacks, purses, food or bottled beverages. They are not permitted on the tour, and there are no lockers on site to store them.

∘ Use the bathroom before arriving, as there are no public facilities at the White House. The closest restroom is at the visitor pavilion.

∘ It's fine to ask the Secret Service members standing guard in each room questions about the house's history and architecture.

✗ Take a Break

Go where the political players go: Old Ebbitt Grill (p66) for burgers, oysters and a nice cabernet sauvignon; or Round Robin (p67) for a mint julep or single-malt Scotch.

East & West Wings

The East and West Wings are on either side of the Residence. In general, the West Wing is the business side, and the East Wing is the social side. So the Situation Room – a 5000-sq-ft complex staffed 24/7 to monitor national and world intelligence information – is in the West Wing. The Cabinet Room is there too, with its huge mahogany table around which the cabinet secretaries sit to discuss business with the president. The East Wing – where the public tours begin – holds the first lady's office, the social secretary's office, and the Graphics and Calligraphy Office (though you won't see any of these).

Personal Touches

Presidents have customized the property over time. Franklin Roosevelt added a pool; Truman gutted the whole place (and simply discarded many of its historical features – today's rooms are replicas); Jacqueline Kennedy brought back antique furnishings and historic details; Nixon added a bowling alley; Carter installed solar roof panels, which Reagan then removed; Clinton added a jogging track; and George W Bush included a T-ball field.

Tours

Tours are free, but they have to be arranged in advance. Americans must apply via one of their state's members of Congress; non-Americans must ask their country's

The presidential podium in the Rose Garden of the White House

embassy in DC for assistance – in reality, there's only a slim chance that the embassy will be able to help source tickets. Applications are taken from 21 days to three months in advance; the earlier you request during this time frame the better. Don't take it personally if you don't get accepted. Capacity is limited, and often official events take precedence over public tours. If you do get in, the self-guided walk-through takes about 30 minutes.

Visitor Center

The **White House Visitor Center**
(☏202-208-1631; www.nps.gov/whho; 1450 Pennsylvania Ave NW, White House Area; admission free; ⊙7:30am-4pm; Ⓜ Orange, Silver, Blue Lines to Federal Triangle) is your backup plan. Browse artifacts such as Roosevelt's desk for his fireside chats and Lincoln's cabinet chair. See the chocolate molds that White House pastry chefs use. Multimedia exhibits give a 360-degree view into the White House's rooms. It's obviously not the same as seeing the real deal first-hand, but the center does do its job very well, giving a comprehensive history sprinkled with great anecdotes on presidential spouses, kids, pets and dinner preferences. Betcha didn't know President Garfield liked squirrel soup? The gift shop is excellent if you're looking for classy souvenirs.

Best Photo Opportunities

Want to snap a selfie with a White House backdrop? You have two options. First head to Pennsylvania Ave, past the peace activists who are always there, for photos across the North Lawn. This view shows the triangular north portico and main driveway. Then walk to E St NW for pictures with a South Lawn background. The view here focuses on the rounded south portico and distant flowery gardens. Alas, there's a security barrier between you and the White House fence, so you won't be getting any unfettered close-ups.

N St NW

M St NW

M St NW

25th St NW

24th St NW

Pennsylvania Ave NW

New Hampshire Ave NW

21st St NW

20th St NW

L St NW

23rd St NW

Rock Creek Park

26th St NW

⊗8

K St NW

Washington Circle

K St NW

19th St NW

27th St NW

26th St NW

Snows Ct

New Hampshire Ave NW

Pennsylvania Ave NW

Foggy Bottom-GWU Ⓜ

I St NW

6⊗

Virginia Ave NW

George Washington University

H St NW

4⊙

Watergate Complex

22nd St NW

21st St NW

University Yard
Textile Museum

⊙2

FOGGY BOTTOM

New Hampshire Ave NW

G St NW

20th St NW

19th St NW

F St NW

Ⓟ

F St NW

New York Ave NW

4

⊕11

E St NW

Rawlins Park

E St NW

23rd St NW

Department of the Interior

5

Rock Creek and Potomac Pkwy NW

New Hampshire Ave NW

22nd St NW

Department of State

Virginia Ave NW

C St NW

C St NW

20th St NW

6

Potomac River

Constitution Ave NW

Constitution Gardens

For reviews see
- ⊙ Top Experiences p58
- ⊙ Sights p64
- ⊗ Eating p66
- 🍷 Drinking p66
- ⭐ Entertainment p67
- 🛍 Shopping p69

E

F

Scott Circle

G

N St NW

H

1

Rhode Island Ave NW

Massachusetts Ave NW

Thomas Circle

M St NW

Connecticut Ave NW

18th St NW

17th St NW

16th St NW

15th St NW

Vermont Ave NW

L St NW

13th St NW

2

Farragut North Ⓜ

K St NW

Farragut Sq

Black Lives Matter Plaza

McPherson Sq

Franklin Sq

Farragut West Ⓜ

Connecticut Ave NW

I St NW

Vermont Ave NW

15th St NW

McPherson Sq Ⓜ

Zei Al NW

H St NW

9 🍴

New York Ave NW

3

1 Renwick Gallery ◎

Lafayette Sq

Treasury Annex

DOWNTOWN

Pennsylvania Ave NW

Ⓟ

13 🔒
14 🔒

G St NW

Ⓟ

Metro Center Ⓜ

G St NW

Old Executive Office Building

White House ◉

17th St NW

Department of the Treasury

15th St NW

🍴 **7**
12 ✴

14th St NW

F St NW

13th St NW

Ⓟ

18th St NW

F St NW

South Lawn

10 🍴

Pennsylvania Ave NW

E St NW

Pennsylvania Ave NW

5 ◎

D St NW

3 ◎ Ellipse

Department of Commerce Building

5

Federal Triangle Ⓜ

12th St NW

Daughters of the American Revolution Museum

Constitution Ave NW

6

NATIONAL MALL

National Mall

E

F

G

H

Food Truck Fiesta

More than 150 food trucks roll in DC, and the White House neighborhood welcomes the mother lode. They congregate at Farragut Sq, Franklin Sq, the State Department and George Washington University on weekdays between 11:30am and 1:30pm. Follow the locals' lead, and stuff your face with a delicious meal for under $15 – maybe a lobster roll poached in butter or a bowl of Lao drunken noodles. **Food Truck Fiesta** (www.foodtruckfiesta. com) tracks the ever-evolving fleet via Twitter.

Sights

Renwick Gallery   MUSEUM

1 MAP P62, E3

Part of the Smithsonian group, the Renwick Gallery is set in a stately 1859 mansion on the same block of Pennsylvania as the White House. It emerged as a showcase for modern and contemporary artists who use innovative techniques and materials, redefining what 'craft' is and taking contemporary arts and crafts in daring new directions. Recent shows include an interactive homage to Burning Man, and 'WONDER,' with nine artists creating site-specific installations.

(202-633-7970; www.renwick.ameri-canart.si.edu; 1661 Pennsylvania Ave NW, White House Area; admission free; 10am-5:30pm; Orange, Silver, Blue Line to Farragut West)

Textile Museum   MUSEUM

2 MAP P62, C4

This gem is the country's only textile museum. Galleries spread over two floors hold exquisite fabrics and carpets. Exhibits revolve around a theme – say Asian textiles depicting dragons or Kuba cloth from the Democratic Republic of the Congo – and rotate a few times a year. Bonus: the museum shares space with George Washington University's trove of historic maps, drawings and ephemera. (202-994-5200; www.museum.gwu.edu; 701 21st St NW; suggested donation $8, children free; 11am-5pm Mon & Fri, to 7pm Wed & Thu, 10am-5pm Sat, 1-5pm Sun; Orange, Silver, Blue Line to Foggy Bottom-GWU)

Ellipse   PARK

3 MAP P62, F5

The expansive, oval-shaped park on the White House's (p58) south side is known as the Ellipse. It's studded with a random collection of monuments, such as the **Zero Milestone** (the marker for highway distances all across the country) and the **Second Division Memorial** (Constitution Ave NW). It also hosts parades and public events such as the lighting of the national Christmas tree. (Constitution Ave, btwn 15th & 17th Sts NW; Ⓜ️Orange, Silver, Blue Line to Federal Triangle)

Watergate Complex

NOTABLE BUILDING

4 👁 MAP P62, A3

Designed by Italian architect Luigi Moretti and DC-based landscape architect Boris Timchenko and constructed between 1963 and 1971, this five-building curvilinear riverfront complex encompasses apartments, fountains, terraces, boutiques, the recently refurbished Watergate Hotel, and the office towers that made 'Watergate' a byword for political scandal here. (2600 Virginia Ave NW; Ⓜ️Orange, Silver, Blue Line to Foggy Bottom-GWU)

Daughters of the American Revolution Museum

MUSEUM

5 👁 MAP P62, E5

This neoclassical behemoth is said to be the largest complex of buildings in the world owned exclusively by women. They own the entire city block! Enter from D St to reach its museum, where you'll find galleries and a series of 'Period Rooms' furnished to reflect how Americans decorated their houses between the late 17th and early 20th centuries. Guided tours from 10am to 2:30pm Monday to Friday and from 9am to 5pm on Saturday. (DAR Museum; 📞202-879-3220; www.dar.org/museum; 1776 D St NW; admission free; ⏰9:30am-4pm Mon-Fri, 9am-5pm Sat; Ⓜ️Orange, Silver, Blue Line to Farragut West)

Food trucks

KIT LEONG/SHUTTERSTOCK ©

White House Area & Foggy Bottom Sights

Eating

Founding Farmers

AMERICAN $$

6 MAP P62, D3

The philosophy here is laudable: majority owned by farmers, this attractive restaurant in the IMF building aspires to serve contemporary American fare made with fresh and sustainable produce. Sadly, the execution of dishes lets the side down, with food being rushed out of the kitchen without sufficient attention to taste or presentation. (202-822-8783; www.wearefoundingfarmers.com; 1924 Pennsylvania Ave NW; breakfast dishes $6-15, mains $12-37; 7am-10pm Mon, to 11pm Tue-Thu, to midnight Fri, 9am-midnight Sat, to 10pm Sun; ; Orange, Silver, Blue Line to Foggy Bottom-GWU or Farragut West)

Old Ebbitt Grill

AMERICAN $$

7 MAP P62, G4

Established in DC in 1856, this legendary tavern has occupied prime real estate near the White House since 1983. Political players and tourists pack into the wood-paneled interior, where thick burgers, succulent steaks and jumbo lump crab cakes are rotated out almost as quickly as the clientele. Pop in for a cocktail and oysters during happy hour. (202-347-4800; www. ebbitt.com; 675 15th St NW, White House Area; mains $18-32; 7:30am-1am Mon-Fri, from 8:30am Sat & Sun, happy hour 3-6pm & 11pm-1am; Red, Orange, Silver, Blue Line to Metro Center)

Marcel's

FRENCH $$$

8 MAP P62, B2

Chef Robert Wiedmaier stays true to classic French techniques while adding contemporary ingredient embellishments. This imparts a certain je ne sais quoi to his daily-changing menu, making dining here extremely enjoyable. Menu options include a four-course vegetarian menu ($85) and a three-course pre-theater menu ($85) with complimentary limousine service to the Kennedy Center at the meal's end. (202-296-1166; www.marcelsdc.com; 2401 Pennsylvania Ave NW; 3-/7-course menus $115/165; 5-10pm Mon-Thu, to 11pm Fri & Sat, 11:30-2:30 & 5-9:30pm Sun; ; Orange, Silver, Blue Line to Foggy Bottom-GWU)

Drinking

Off the Record

BAR

9 MAP P62, F3

Table seating, an open fire in winter and a discreet basement location in one of the city's most prestigious **hotels** (202-638-6600; www.hayadams.com; 800 16th St NW, White House Area; d from $400; ; Orange, Silver, Blue Line to McPherson Sq), right across from the White House – it's no wonder DC's important people submerge to be seen and not heard (as the tagline goes) here. Experienced bartenders swirl martinis and manhattans for the suit-wearing crowd. Enter through the hotel lobby. (202-638-6600; www.

hayadams.com/dining/off-the-record; 800 16th St NW, Hay-Adams Hotel, White House Area; ⏰11:30am-midnight Sun-Thu, to 12:30am Fri & Sat; Ⓜ Orange, Silver, Blue Line to McPherson Sq)

Round Robin

BAR

10 Ⓔ MAP P62, G4

Dispensing drinks since 1847, the bar at the Willard hotel is one of DC's most famous. The small, circular space is done up in classic accents, all dark wood trim, marble bar and leather seats. While it's touristy, you'll likely still see officials here determining your latest tax hike over a mint julep or single malt scotch. (🖉202-628-9100; http://washington.intercontinental.com/food-drink/round-robin-bar; 1401 Pennsylvania Ave NW, Willard InterContinental Hotel, White House Area; ⏰noon-1am Mon-Sat, to midnight Sun; Ⓜ Red, Orange, Silver, Blue Line to Metro Center)

Entertainment

Kennedy Center

PERFORMING ARTS

11 ⭐ MAP P62, A4

Overlooking the Potomac River, the magnificent Kennedy Center hosts a staggering array of performances – more than 2000 each year in venues including the Concert Hall, home to the **National Symphony** (www.kennedy-center.org/nso; 2700 F St NW, Kennedy Center, Foggy Bottom; Ⓜ Orange, Silver, Blue Line to Foggy Bottom-GWU), and Opera House, home to the **National Opera** (www.kennedy-center.org/wno; 2700 F St NW, Kennedy Center, Foggy Bottom; Ⓜ Orange, Silver, Blue Line to Foggy Bottom-GWU). Free

The Kennedy Center

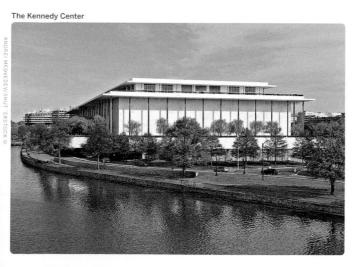

Why Washington, DC?

Where North Meets South

Following the Revolutionary War, the fledgling US Congress set up a temporary capital in Philadelphia while searching for a more permanent home. The Constitution, ratified in 1788, specified that a federal territory, no greater than 10 sq miles, should be established for the nation's capital. Northerners and Southerners both wanted the capital in their territory, and archrivals Thomas Jefferson (a Virginian) and Alexander Hamilton (a New Yorker) struck a compromise, agreeing to construct a new city on the border between north and south. The precise location was left up to the newly inaugurated and wildly popular President George Washington.

Washington chose a site some 20 miles from his own Mount Vernon estate – a place he loved and knew well. The site on the Potomac proved a strategic location for commerce and river traffic, and was politically pleasing to both Northern and Southern concerns. Maryland and Virginia agreed to cede land to the new capital.

A Territory Is Born

Over drinks at Suter's tavern in Georgetown, Washington persuaded local landowners to sell their holdings to the government for $66 an acre. In March 1791 surveyors mapped out a diamond-shaped territory that spanned the Potomac and Anacostia Rivers. Its four corners were at the cardinal points of the compass. Pierre Charles L'Enfant, a French officer in the Revolutionary War, sketched plans for a grand European-style capital of monumental buildings and majestic boulevards. It was named the Territory of Columbia (to honor Christopher Columbus), while the federal city within would be called 'the city of Washington.'

Build & Rebuild

In 1793 construction began on the President's House and the Capitol. In 1800 John Adams became the first president to occupy the mansion, and Congress convened in Washington for the first time. The new plan was going swimmingly until the War of 1812, when the British torched the city. DC was slow to recover. A congressional initiative to abandon the dispirited capital was lost by just nine votes.

It wasn't until the 1860s, when the federal government expanded to administer the Civil War and deal with its aftermath, that the city really came into its own.

performances are staged on the Millennium Stage daily at 6pm as part of the center's 'Performing Arts for Everyone' initiative. (📞20 2-467-4600; www.kennedy-center.org; 2700 F St NW, Foggy Bottom; 🕐box office 10am-9pm Mon-Sat, noon-9pm Sun; 🛜♿; Ⓜ Orange, Silver, Blue Line to Foggy Bottom-GWU)

Hamilton   LIVE MUSIC

12 ⭐ MAP P62, G4

There's lots on offer here. On the ground floor there's a popular restaurant and three bars, one of which offers free live music Thursday, Friday and Saturday nights. In the basement is Hamilton LIVE, a 700-person club that genre-jumps from funk to blues to alt-rock. (📞202-787-1000; www.thehamiltondc. com; 600 14th St NW; Ⓜ Red, Orange, Silver, Blue Line to Metro Center)

Shopping

White House Gifts   GIFTS & SOUVENIRS

13 🔒 MAP P62, G4

Not to be confused with the official White House **gift shop** (http:// shop.whitehousehistory.org; 1450 Pennsylvania Ave NW; 🕐7:30am-4pm; Ⓜ Orange, Silver, Blue Line to Federal Triangle) in the White House Visitor Center, this store sells official souvenirs alongside less-orthodox offerings. So while you can still find the certified White House Christmas ornament among the stock, you'll also see the Political Inaction Figures paper-doll set. (📞20

Kennedy Center Freebies

Don't have the dough for a big-ticket show? No worries. The Kennedy Center's **Millennium Stage** (www.kennedy-center. org/millennium) puts on a first-rate free music or dance performance at 6pm in the Grand Foyer. Check the website to see who's playing.

Guides also offer free, 45-minute tours of the Kennedy's art-filled complex. They depart every 10 minutes from 10am to 5pm Monday to Friday and until 1pm weekends, and take you into all the theaters as well as onto the viewtastic rooftop terrace.

2-737-9500; www.whitehousegifts. com; 701 15th St NW, White House Area; 🕐8am-9pm Mon-Sat, 9am-8pm Sun May-Dec, 9am-8pm Mon-Sat, to 6pm Sun Jan-Apr; Ⓜ Red, Orange, Silver, Blue Line to Metro Center)

W Curtis Draper Tobacconist   CIGARS

14 🔒 MAP P62, G4

Follow your nose into W Curtis Draper, which has been selling cigars to politicos since 1887. Staff are friendly and helpful to stogie-smoking newbies. (📞202-638-2555; www.wcurtisdraper.com; 699 15th St NW; 🕐9:30am-6:30pm Mon-Fri, 10am-4pm Sat; Ⓜ Red, Orange, Silver, Blue Line to Metro Center)

Explore

Georgetown

Georgetown is DC's most aristocratic neighborhood, home to elite university students, ivory-tower academics and diplomats. Shopaholics have chic boutiques, hikers and cyclists have idyllic trails, and garden lovers have genteel landscapes to stroll through. Upscale cafes and dark-wood pubs invite lingering into the night.

The Short List

○ **Dumbarton Oaks (p75)** *Meandering the ponds, pools and terraced formal gardens outside, then heading inside to peruse El Greco art, pre-Columbian ceramics and the library of centuries-old books.*

○ **C&O Canal Towpath (p75)** *Escaping the concrete jungle by walking or cycling the bucolic path, going far enough to see wooden bridges and vintage lock houses.*

○ **Georgetown Waterfront Park (p73)** *Sipping an alfresco drink and watching rowers skim the Potomac.*

○ **Key Bridge Boathouse (p75)** *Paddling past DC's stony monuments on a sunset tour.*

○ **Martin's Tavern (p73)** *Swirling a cocktail in the same room where JFK proposed to Jackie.*

Getting There & Around

Ⓜ The Foggy Bottom-GWU stop (Orange, Silver, Blue Lines) is a 0.75-mile walk from M St's edge.

🚍 The DC Circulator's Dupont–Georgetown–Rosslyn line runs from the Dupont Circle Metro station (south entrance), with stops along M St. The Union Station–Georgetown line runs via K St and Wisconsin Ave.

🚶 A half-mile riverside path connects Georgetown Waterfront Park to the Kennedy Center.

Neighborhood Map on p74

Copley Hall at Georgetown University (p76) KIT LEONG/GETTYIMAGES ©

Walking Tour 🥾

Strolling Genteel Georgetown

If ever a neighborhood was prime for ambling, it's Georgetown, in all its leafy, filigreed-manor glory. The area has always been Washington's poshest place. A wander through reveals grand row houses, swanky antique shops, indulgent patisseries and university rowing crews, along with hot spots related to John F Kennedy and Jackie.

Start Book Hill

Finish Georgetown Waterfront Park

Length 1 mile

Metro Circulator Georgetown Union Station

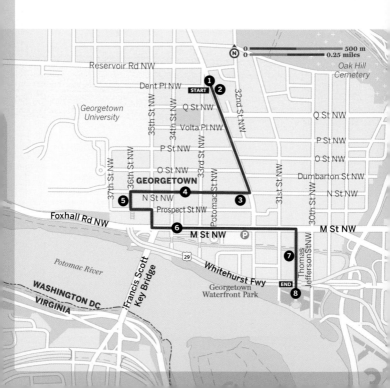

❶ Book Hill Antiques

Book Hill is a Paris-like row of art galleries, interior-design stores and antique shops that slopes down the 1600 block of Wisconsin Ave.

❷ Croissants at Patisserie Poupon

The society ladies know where to replenish mid-shopping spree: **Patisserie Poupon** (www.patisseriepoupon.net; 1645 Wisconsin Ave NW; baked goods $3-5, mains $8-14; ⏱8:30am-6pm Tue-Fri, 8am-5:30pm Sat, to 4pm Sun; 🚌Circulator). Join them in nibbling almond croissants or drinking French-press coffee.

❸ Martin's Tavern à la Jack & Jackie

John F Kennedy proposed to Jackie in Booth 3 at **Martin's Tavern** (www.martinstavern.com; 1264 Wisconsin Ave NW; mains $18-34; ⏱11am-1:30am Mon-Thu, to 2:30am Fri, 8am-2:30am Sat, 8am-1:30am Sun). Georgetown's oldest saloon remains a favorite with students and senators alike, who appreciate the warm, dark-wood ambience.

❹ N Street Style

Walk on tree-shaded N St and you'll see the neighborhood's typical Federal-style row houses. With $1 million or so you can buy one of the historic beauties. JFK and Jackie once lived at 3307 N St.

❺ Drinks at the Tombs

If it looks familiar, think back to the '80s: the **Tombs** (www.tombs.com; 1226 36th St NW; ⏱11:30am-1:30am Mon-Thu, to 2:30am Fri, 11am-2:30am Sat, 9:30am-1:30am Sun) was the setting for the film *St Elmo's Fire*. Today the cozy, subterranean pub is a favorite with Georgetown students and teaching assistants.

❻ M Street Shop-a-thon

M St is Georgetown's main vein where the young and fashionable come to shop. Upscale brand-name stores mix it up with designer consignment boutiques.

❼ Baked & Wired Refuel

Sniff out **Baked & Wired** (www.bakedandwired.com; 1052 Thomas Jefferson St NW; baked goods $3-8; ⏱7am-8pm Mon-Thu, to 9pm Fri, 8am-9pm Sat, 8am-8pm Sun), a cheery cafe that whips up beautifully made coffees and monster cupcakes.

❽ People-Watching at the Park

Georgetown Waterfront Park This park (www.georgetownwaterfrontpark.org; Water St NW/K St, btwn 31st St NW & Key Bridge; 🚶; 🚌Circulator Georgetown-Union Station) is a favorite with couples, families and power players showing off their big yachts. Benches dot the way, where you can sit and watch the rowing teams out on the Potomac River.

Georgetown

For reviews see
- ◎ Sights p75
- ✕ Eating p77
- 🍴 Drinking p78
- ✪ Entertainment p78
- 🛍 Shopping p78

Sights

Dumbarton Oaks GARDENS, MUSEUM

1  MAP P74, E1

The mansion's 27 acres of enchanting formal gardens are straight out of a storybook. The springtime blooms are stunning. The mansion itself is worth a visit to see exquisite Byzantine and pre-Columbian art (including El Greco's *The Visitation*) and the fascinating library of rare books that date as far back as 1491. From November to mid-March the gardens are free. Enter them at R and 31st Sts NW. (☎202-339-6400; www.doaks.org; 1703 32nd St NW; museum free, gardens adult/child $10/5; ⏱museum 11:30am-5:30pm Tue-Sun, gardens 2-6pm; 🚌Circulator Georgetown-Union Station)

C&O Canal Towpath CYCLING, HIKING

2  MAP P74, E3

This shaded hiking-cycling path runs alongside a waterway built in the mid-1800s to transport goods to West Virginia. Step on at Jefferson St for a lovely escape from the crowds. (www.nps.gov/choh; 1057 Thomas Jefferson St NW, visitor center; 🚌Circulator Georgetown-Union Station)

Key Bridge Boathouse WATER SPORTS

3  MAP P74, C3

Located beneath the Key Bridge, the boathouse rents canoes, kayaks and stand up paddleboards (prices start at $16 per hour). In summer it also offers guided,

Georgetown Sights

Dumbarton Oaks House and Gardens

KARSTEN JUNG/SHUTTERSTOCK ©

90-minute kayak trips ($45 per person) that glide past the Lincoln Memorial as the sun sets. If you have a bike, the boathouse is a mere few steps from the **Capital Crescent Trail** (www.cctrail.org; Water St; ⧉ Circulator Georgetown-Union Station). (☏ 202-337-9642; www.boatingindc.com/boathouses/key-bridge-boathouse; 3500 Water St NW; ☉ hours vary mid-Apr–Oct; ⧉ Circulator Georgetown-Union Station)

Big Wheel Bikes CYCLING

4 ◉ MAP P74, D3

Big Wheel has a wide variety of two-wheelers to rent, and you can spin onto the C&O Canal Towpath (p75) practically from the front door. Staff members also provide the lowdown on the nearby Capital Crescent Trail and **Mount Vernon Trail** (www.nps.gov; ☉ 6am-10pm; Ⓜ Arlington Cemetery, Ronald Reagan Washington National Airport & Rosslyn). There's a three-hour minimum with rentals. For an extra $10 you can keep your bike overnight. (☏ 202-337-0254; www.bigwheelbikes.com; 1034 33rd St NW; per 3hr/day $21/35; ☉ 11am-7pm Tue-Fri, 10am-6pm Sat & Sun; ⧉ Circulator)

Georgetown University UNIVERSITY

5 ◉ MAP P74, C2

Georgetown is one of the nation's top universities, with a student body that's equally hard-working and hard-partying. Founded in 1789, it was America's first Roman Catholic university. Notable alumni include Bill Clinton, as well as many international royals and heads of state. Near the campus' east gate, medieval-looking **Healy Hall** (Georgetown University; ⧉ Circulator) impresses with its tall, Hogwarts-esque clock tower. Pretty **Dalghren Chapel** (Georgetown University; ⧉ Circulator) and its quiet courtyard hide behind it. (☏ 202-687-0100; www.georgetown.edu; cnr 37th & O Sts NW; ⧉ Circulator Georgetown-Union Station)

Exorcist Stairs FILM LOCATION

6 ◉ MAP P74, C2

The steep set of stairs dropping down to M St is a popular track for joggers, but more famously it's the spot where demonically possessed Father Karras tumbles to his death in horror-film classic *The Exorcist* (1973). Come on foggy nights, when the stone steps really are creepy as hell. (3600 Prospect St NW; ⧉ Circulator Georgetown-Union Station)

Tudor Place MUSEUM

7 ◉ MAP P74, E1

This 1816 neoclassical mansion was owned by Thomas Peter and Martha Custis Peter, the granddaughter of Martha Washington, and lived in by six generations of her family. Today the manor functions as a small museum, featuring family furnishings and artwork, which give a good insight into American decorative arts. The grand, five-acre gardens bloom with roses, lilies, poplar trees and exotic palms. (☏ 202-965-0400; www.tudorplace.org; 1644 31st St

NW; 1hr house tour adult/child $10/3, self-guided garden tour $3; ⊙10am-4pm Tue-Sat, from noon Sun, closed Jan; ⊒Circulator Georgetown-Union Station)

Old Stone House HISTORIC SITE

8 MAP P74, E3

Built in 1766 in what was then the British colony of Maryland, the capital's oldest surviving building has been a tavern, a brothel and a boardinghouse (sometimes all at once). Today it's a small museum offering a peek into Revolutionary War-era life. (www.nps.gov; 3051 M St NW; admission free; ⊙11am-6pm; ⊒Circulator Georgetown-Union Station)

Eating

Simply Banh Mi VIETNAMESE $

9 MAP P74, D1

There's nothing fancy about this small space, and its compact menu sticks mostly to sandwiches and bubble tea. But the brother-sister owners know how to take a crusty baguette, stuff it with delicious lemongrass pork or other meat (or tofu), and make your day (✐20 2-333-5726; www.simplybanhmidc.com; 1624 Wisconsin Ave NW; mains $7-10; ⊙11am-7pm Sun, Tue & Wed, to 9pm Thu-Sat; ✐; ⊒Circulator Georgetown-Union Station)

Il Canale ITALIAN $$$

10 MAP P74, E3

Real-deal Neapolitan pizza emerges from the real-deal, Italian wood-

Dumbarton Oaks Park

Next door to Dumbarton Oaks garden, **Dumbarton Oaks Park** (www.dopark.org; Lovers' Lane; ⊙sunrise-sunset; ⊒Circulator) was once part of the estate but is now a public woodland beloved by joggers and dog walkers. Access it via Lovers' Lane and enter a world of forested trails, quaint stone bridges, mini waterfalls and deer-filled meadows.

fired oven in Il Canale's bouncy town-house digs. It's casual and low-cost for Georgetown, which is why families, couples and groups of friends pile in at all hours. (✐20 2-337-4444; www.ilcanale.com; 1065 31st St NW; mains $23-32; ⊙11:30am-10:30pm Mon-Thu, to 11pm Fri & Sat, to 10pm Sun; ⊒Circulator Georgetown-Union Station)

Fiola Mare SEAFOOD $$$

11 MAP P74, E4

Fiola Mare delivers the chichi Georgetown experience. It receives fresh fish and crustaceans daily. The yacht-bobbling river view rocks. The see-and-be-seen multitudes are here. It's DC at its luxe best. Make reservations. (✐202-628-0065; www.fiolamaredc.com; 3050 K St NW, Washington Harbour; mains $28-54; ⊙5-10pm Mon, 11:30am-2:30pm & 5-10pm Tue-Fri, 11:30am-2pm & 5-10:30pm Sat, 11am-2pm & 5-10pm Sun; ⊒Circulator)

Chez Billy Sud
FRENCH $$$

12 🍴 MAP P74, E3

An endearing little bistro tucked away on a residential block, Billy's exudes laid-back elegance. Mustachioed servers bring baskets of warm bread to the white-linen-clothed tables, along with crispy moulard duck leg, Maine mussels, and plump cream puffs. (📞202-965-2606; www.chezbillysud.com; 1039 31st St NW; mains $25-38; ⏰5-10pm Mon, 11:30am-2pm & 5-10pm Tue-Thu, 11:30am-2pm & 5-11pm Fri, 11am-2pm & 5-11pm Sat, 11am-2pm & 5-10pm Sun; 🚃Circulator Georgetown-Union Station)

Cafe Milano
ITALIAN $$$

13 🍴 MAP P74, E2

Milano has been reeling in the political glitterati for years with its executions of northern Italian favorites. Be prepared to pay for the European-chic ambience and celebrity-spotting. The pastas get the biggest praise. (📞202-333-6183; www.cafemilano.com; 3251 Prospect St NW; mains $25-55; ⏰11:30am-11pm Mon & Tue, to midnight Wed-Sat, 11am-11pm Sun; 🚃Circulator)

Drinking

Ching Ching Cha
TEAHOUSE

14 ☕ MAP P74, E3

Airy, Zen-like Ching Ching Cha is a world away from the shopping mayhem of M St. Stop in for a leisurely pot of tea and snacks such as steamed dumplings, coconut tarts, or a 'tea meal,' with three little dishes along the lines of green squash and miso salmon. (📞202-333-8288; www.chingching-cha.com; 1063 Wisconsin Ave NW; ⏰11am-8pm Thu-Mon; 🚃Circulator)

Cafe Bonaparte
CAFE

15 ☕ MAP P74, D1

This jewel-box cafe feels as though it has been plucked straight from the streets of Paris. Come to sip a café au lait or a glass of sparkling wine. Hopefully you're not in a hurry, because service can be slow. (📞202-333-8830; www.cafebonaparte.com; 1522 Wisconsin Ave NW; ⏰9am-10pm Mon-Thu & Sun, to 11pm Fri, 10am-11pm Sat; 🚃Circulator)

Entertainment

Blues Alley
JAZZ

16 ⭐ MAP P74, E3

Greats like Dizzy Gillespie and Sarah Vaughan played this venerable club back in the day. The talent remains just as sterling now, and the setting just as sophisticated. There's a $12 minimum purchase requirement once you're seated. (📞202-337-4141; www.bluesalley.com; 1073 Wisconsin Ave NW; tickets from $20; ⏰shows 8pm & 10pm; 🚃Circulator)

Shopping

Oliver Dunn, Moss & Co
ANTIQUES

17 🔒 MAP P74, D1

The lengthy name comes from two businesses under one roof. Located in a cute row house in the thick of Book Hill (Georgetown's antique-laden block of shops), this spot spreads posh linens, Scandinavian textiles, French signs and concrete garden ornaments through six rooms and a back yard. (📞202-338-7410; 1657 Wisconsin Ave NW; ⏰11am-5pm Tue-Sat; 🚌Circulator)

Tugooh Toys

TOYS

18 🔒 MAP P74, E2

If you've ever been nostalgic for the great wooden toys of childhood, this hip wonderland has the goods with clever modern touches. Lots of eco-friendly playthings and educational games stack the shelves, too. (📞202-338-9476; www.tugoohtoys.com; 1355 Wisconsin Ave NW; ⏰11am-5pm Mon-Thu, to 6pm Fri, 10am-6pm Sat, to 5pm Sun; 🚌Circulator) d

Grace Street Coffee

🍽️

Little **Grace Street Coffee** (📞202-470-1331; www.gracestcoffee.com; 3210 Grace St NW; ⏰7am-5pm Mon-Thu, to 6pm Fri-Sun; 🚌Circulator) roasts its own beans and makes its own syrups, and then morphs them into exquisite coffee drinks. It's in a mini food hall that shares space with a juice bar and top-notch sandwich shop (called Sundevich, which specializes in creations named after global cities, like the chicken-and-avocado Lima and the gruyere-and-ham Paris). Lots of hip locals relax over a cup here.

Fiola Mare (p77)

KRISTI BLOKHIN/SHUTTERSTOCK ©

Explore
Capitol Hill

This vast area holds top sights such as the domed Capitol and US Holocaust Memorial Museum, but creaky bookshops and cozy pubs also thrive here. The areas around Eastern Market and H St NE are locals' hubs, with good-time restaurants and nightlife.

The Short List

○ **US Capitol (p82)** *Counting the statues, ogling the frescoes, eating the bean soup and visiting the chambers of the guys and gals who run the country.*

○ **United States Holocaust Memorial Museum (p84)** *Immersing yourself in the good and bad sides of human nature.*

○ **Library of Congress (p90)** *Being wowed by the sheer volume of, well, volumes, then discovering ancient maps and cartoons in the exhibition rooms.*

○ **Supreme Court (p90)** *Listening in on case arguments and watching the black-robed justices in action.*

Getting There & Away

Ⓜ Union Station (Red Line), Capitol South (Orange, Silver and Blue), Eastern Market (Orange, Silver and Blue) and Navy Yard (Green) are the main stations. The Wharf is equidistant to two stops: L'Enfant Plaza (Orange, Silver, Blue, Yellow and Green) and Waterfront (Green).

Streetcar DC's free new line zips along H St from Union Station to 15th St. Catch it behind Union Station (follow the streetcar signs through the terminal, past all the buses). It stops at 3rd St, 5th St, 8th St, 13th St and 15th St.

Neighborhood Map on p88

The Capitol Building (p82) S-F/SHUTTERSTOCK ©

Top Experience 📸

Take in the Grandeur of the US Capitol

The political center of the US government and geographic heart of the District, the US Capitol sits atop a high hill overlooking the National Mall and the wide avenues flaring out to the city beyond. The towering 288ft cast-iron dome, ornate fountains and marble Roman pillars set on sweeping lawns scream: 'This is DC.'

◎ MAP P88, D3

www.visitthecapitol.gov

1st St SE & E Capitol St, Capitol Hill

admission free

🕗8:30am-4:30pm Mon-Sat

Ⓜ Orange, Silver, Blue Line to Capitol South

Capitol Visitor Center & Tours

The **Capitol Visitor Center** (☎202-226-8000; www.visitthecapitol.gov; 1st St NE & E Capitol St; ☺8:30am-4:30pm Mon-Sat; Ⓜ Orange, Silver, Blue Lines to Capitol South) sits below the East Plaza and is where all visits begin. Tours are free, but you need a ticket. Get one at the information desk, or reserve online in advance (there's no fee). The hour-long jaunt starts with a cheesy film about how the US government works. Then staff members lead you into the ornate halls and whispery chambers.

Rotunda

The Capitol's centerpiece is the magnificent Rotunda (the area under the dome). It's 96ft in diameter and 180ft high. A Constantino Brumidi frieze around the rim replays more than 400 years of American history. Look up into the eye of the dome for the *Apotheosis of Washington,* an allegorical fresco by Brumidi.

Statues

The Capitol also contains sculptures of two famous residents per state. Many of these are found in the Hall of Statues. You might recognize likenesses of George Washington (Virginia) and Ronald Reagan (California), less so Uriah Milton Rose (Arkansas). After the tour, swing by the Exhibition Hall and check out the plaster model for the *Statue of Freedom* that crowns the dome.

Military Bands

The Army, Navy, Marine Corps and Air Force bands take turns performing on the steps of the Capitol on weekdays (except Thursday) June through August. Look for them at 8pm on the West Front.

★ Top Tips

o Between March and August, it's wise to reserve tours online.

o Note you cannot bring any food or drinks inside the building.

o The Visitor Center offers several free apps on the Capitol grounds, statues, and more. Download them at www.visit-thecapitol.gov

o To reach the Supreme Court and Library of Congress easily, take the underground tunnel from the Capitol.

✕ Take a Break

Jimmy T's (501 E Capitol St SE, Capitol Hill; mains $6-10; ☺6:30am-3pm Tue, Fri & Sat, to 4pm Wed, to 6pm Thu, 8am-3pm Sun; 👶🐾; Ⓜ Orange, Silver, Blue Line to Eastern Market) is an old-school diner, four blocks from the Capitol, where locals come for omelets and coffee; cash only.

Good Stuff Eatery (p92) is also nearby for foodie-style burgers and milkshakes.

Top Experience

Absorb History at the United States Holocaust Memorial Museum

For a deep understanding of the Holocaust, this harrowing museum is a must-see. It gives visitors the identity card of a single Holocaust victim, whose story gets revealed as you plunge into a past marked by ghettos, rail cars and death camps. It also shows the flip side of human nature, documenting the risks many citizens took to help the persecuted.

⦿ MAP P88, A4

www.ushmm.org

100 Raoul Wallenberg Pl

admission free

🕐 10am-5:20pm,

Ⓜ Orange, Silver, Blue Line to Smithsonian

Hall of Witness & Skylight

James Ingo Freed designed the extraordinary building in 1993, and its stark facade and steel-and-glass interior echo the death camps themselves. Look up at the skylight in the Hall of Witness when you enter the building. Many survivors say this reminds them of the sky above the camps. For them it was symbolic: the only thing the Nazis couldn't control.

Nazi Assault

The permanent exhibit presents the Holocaust's history chronologically in galleries spanning three floors. It starts on the 4th floor, which is titled 'Nazi Assault' and covers the period between 1933 and 1939. Watch propaganda films of Hitler, Goebbels and others, and learn how the Nazis used then modern technology, such as film, to craft their message to sway citizens.

Final Solution & Last Chapter

The 3rd floor is 'The Final Solution,' covering the period between 1940 and 1945. Here you'll see a rail car used to transport people to the camps, a wooden bunk bed from Auschwitz and a scale model of Crematorium II at Auschwitz. The 2nd floor is the 'Last Chapter,' where old film footage shows their liberation from camps, and videos illuminate individual survivors telling their stories.

Hall of Remembrance & Wexner Center

As you exit the permanent exhibit, you come out into the candlelit Hall of Remembrance, a sanctuary for quiet reflection. The Wexner Center is likewise on this floor, and features exhibits on other genocides around the world.

★ Top Tips

o Same-day passes to view the permanent exhibit are required March through August, available at the pass desk on the 1st floor. The passes allow entrance at a designated time. Arrive early because they do run out.

o Better yet, reserve tickets in advance via the museum's website for a $1 surcharge.

o If you have children under 11 years, a gentler installation – 'Remember the Children: Daniel's Story' – is on the 1st floor.

✗ Take a Break

Follow your nose to the Maine Avenue Fish Market (p92) and a feast of blue crabs and chowder. It's about 0.75 miles southeast of the museum.

Hop on the Metro to Eastern Market (p87), where cheese, fruit, baked goods and other picnic fixings await.

Walking Tour 🥾

A Capital Day on Capitol Hill

Pretend you're a resident of one of the brown-stone homes along the red-brick sidewalks and shop for seafood at Eastern Market or browse the Flea Market's curios. Have breakfast anytime in a dive bar, then stop by the rambling, double-stacked bookshop. Share small plates and drinks with friends, and wave to neighbors at the riverside park.

Start Tune Inn
Finish Yards Park
Length 1.5 miles
Metro Orange, Silver, Blue Line to Eastern Market

❶ The Dive Bar: Tune Inn

Tune Inn (331 Pennsylvania Ave SE, Capitol Hill; ⏰8am-2am Sun-Thu, to 3am Fri & Sat; Ⓜ️Orange, Silver, Blue Line to Capitol South or Eastern Market) has been around for decades. The mounted deer heads and antler chandelier set the mood, as greasy-spoon grub and all-day breakfasts get served.

❷ Capitol Hill Books

Rambling **Capitol Hill Books** (www.capitolhillbooks-dc.com; 657 C St SE, Capitol Hill; ⏰10am-8pm Mon-Fri, from 9am Sat & Sun, to 7pm Sun;) has so many used tomes they're stacked two deep on the shelves. Floors creak and classical music plays as neighborhood bibliophiles sift through the whopping selection.

❸ Eastern Market

Eastern Market (www.easternmarket-dc.org; 225 7th St SE, Capitol Hill; ⏰7am-7pm Tue-Fri, to 6pm Sat, 9am-5pm Sun) is the true heart of Capitol Hill. Vendors selling baked goods, cheeses, meats and seafood fill the covered arcade. At the weekend, the market spills onto the street.

❹ Flea Market Finds

On weekends the **Flea Market** (www.easternmarket.net; 7th St SE, btwn C St & Penn Ave; ⏰10am-5pm Sat & Sun;) sets up in the street adjacent to Eastern Market, doubling the browsing acreage. Vendors sell cool art, antiques, furniture, maps, prints, clothing and curios.

❺ Street Art at the Fridge

First you have to find the **Fridge** (www.instagram.com/thefridgedc; 516½ 8th St SE, rear alley; admission free; ⏰1-7pm Thu & Fri, noon-7pm Sat, noon-5pm Sun), a friendly gallery specializing in street art. Follow the murals into the alley across 8th St from Ambar restaurant.

❻ Meet Friends at Ambar

Ambar (www.ambarrestaurant.com; 523 8th St SE, Capitol Hill; small plates $7-13; ⏰11am-2:30pm & 4-10pm Mon-Thu, 11am-2:30pm & 4-11pm Fri, 10am-3:30pm & 4:30-11pm Sat, 10am-3:30pm & 4:30-10pm Sun) buzzes when the convivial restaurant slings heaps of small plates. Roasted pepper and eggplant, lamb salami, brandy-soaked mussels – tables of friends share intriguing Balkan dishes.

❼ Dinner at Rose's Luxury

Locals line up for shabby-chic **Rose's Luxury** (www.rosesluxury.com; 717 8th St SE, Capitol Hill; small plates $14-16, family plates $33-36; ⏰5-10pm Mon-Sat), which offers a changing menu of 10 or so plates a day.

❽ River Views at Yards Park

Lovely **Yards Park** (www.capitolriverfront.org/yards-park; 355 Water St SE; ⏰7am-2hr past sunset) is a sculpted public space with a wooden boardwalk, excellent river view and a funky modernist bridge.

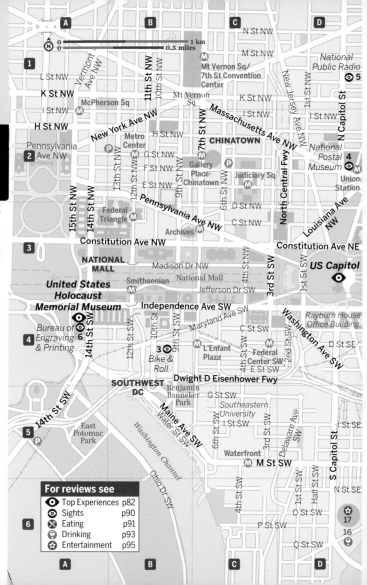

Capitol Hill

N St NW

M St NW

L St NW

K St NW

I St NW

H St NW

Vermont Ave NW

McPherson Sq

Pennsylvania Ave NW

11th St NW

10th St NW

Mt Vernon Sq

Mt Vernon Sq/ 7th St Convention Center

New York Ave NW

Metro Center

Federal Triangle

H St NW

G St NW

F St NW

E St NW

7th St NW

Gallery Place-Chinatown

Pennsylvania Ave NW

Archives

K St NW

I St NW

CHINATOWN

Massachusetts Ave NW

Judiciary Sq

D St NW

C St NW

New Jersey Ave NW

North Central Fwy

National Public Radio

National Postal Museum

Union Station

1st St NE

N Capitol St

Louisiana Ave NW

Constitution Ave NW

Constitution Ave NE

15th St NW

14th St NW

13th St NW

12th St NW

NATIONAL MALL

United States Holocaust Memorial Museum

Bureau of Engraving & Printing

14th St SW

Madison Dr NW

Smithsonian

Independence Ave SW

10th St

12th St SW

Bike & Roll

SOUTHWEST DC

National Mall

Jefferson Dr SW

Maryland Ave SW

L'Enfant Plaza

Dwight D Eisenhower Fwy

Benjamin Banneker Park

4th St SW

3rd SW

C St SW

D St SW

E St SW

G St SW

Southeastern University

I St SW

US Capitol

1st St SW

Washington Ave SW

Rayburn House Office Building

D St SE

Federal Center SW

2nd St SW

Maine Ave SW

Water St SW

Washington Channel

East Potomac Park

Ohio Dr SW

6th St SW

Delaware Ave

Waterfront

M St SW

1st St SW

S Capitol St

3rd St SW

2nd St SW

1st St SW

Half St SW

N St SW

O St SW

4th St SW

P St SW

Q St SW

17

16

For reviews see

◉ Top Experiences p82
◎ Sights p90
✗ Eating p91
🍷 Drinking p93
★ Entertainment p95

Sights

Library of Congress
LIBRARY

1 ⊙ MAP P88, E4

The world's largest library – with 164 million books, manuscripts, maps, photos, films and other items – awes in both scope and design. The centerpiece is the 1897 **Jefferson Building**. Gawk at the **Great Hall**, done up in stained glass, marble and mosaics of mythical characters, then seek out the **Gutenberg Bible** (c 1455), Thomas Jefferson's round library and the reading room viewing area. Free tours of the building take place between 10:30am and 3:30pm on the half-hour. (📞20 2-707-8000; www.loc.gov; 10 1st St SE, Capitol Hill; admission free; ⊘8:30am-4:30pm Mon-Sat; Ⓜ Orange, Silver, Blue Line to Capitol South)

Supreme Court
LANDMARK

2 ⊙ MAP P88, E3

The highest court in the USA occupies a pseudo-Greek temple protected by 13,000lb bronze doors. Arrive early to watch arguments (periodic Monday through Wednesday from October to April). You can visit the permanent exhibits and the building's two five-story, marble-and-bronze spiral staircases year-round. On days when court is not in session you can also hear lectures (on the half-hour) in the courtroom. Be sure to exit via the doors that lead to the regal front steps. (📞202-479-3000; www.supremecourt.gov; 1 1st St NE, Capitol Hill; admission free; ⊘9am-4:30pm Mon-Fri; Ⓜ Orange, Silver, Blue Line to Capitol South)

Bike & Roll
CYCLING

3 ⊙ MAP P88, B4

This branch of the bike-rental company (from $16 per two hours) is the one closest to the Mall. In addition to bike rental, it also provides tours. Three-hour jaunts wheel by the main sights of Capitol Hill and the National Mall. The evening rides to the monuments are particularly good. (📞202-842-2453; www.bikeandrolldc.com; 955 L'Enfant Plaza SW, South DC; tours adult/child from $44/34; ⊘9am-8pm, reduced hours spring & fall, closed early Jan–mid-Mar; Ⓜ Orange, Silver, Blue, Yellow, Green Line to L'Enfant Plaza)

National Postal Museum
MUSEUM

4 ⊙ MAP P88, D2

The Smithsonian-run Postal Museum is way cooler than it sounds. Level 1 has exhibits on postal history from the Pony Express to modern times, where you'll see antique mail planes and touching old letters from soldiers and pioneers. Level 2 holds the world's largest stamp collection. Join the stamp geeks snapping photos of the world's rarest stamps, or start your own collection, with thousands of free international stamps. (📞202-633-5555; www.postalmuseum.si.edu; 2 Massachusetts Ave NE; admission free; ⊘10am-5:30pm; 🚻; Ⓜ Red Line to Union Station)

National Public Radio

NOTABLE BUILDING

5 ⊙ MAP P88, D1

Fans of *Morning Edition* and *All Things Considered* can see where the magic happens at National Public Radio's ecofriendly headquarters. Hour-long tours peek into the newsroom and a high-tech production studio. The guides – usually former employees – entertain with insider stories. Reservations required. The on-site shop sells nifty gifts such as the Nina Totin' bag (named for longtime reporter Nina Totenberg). (📞202-513-2000; http://tours.npr.org; 1111 N Capitol St NE; admission free; ⏰tours 11am Mon-Fri; Ⓜ Red Line to NoMa)

Bureau of Engraving & Printing

LANDMARK

6 ⊙ MAP P88, A4

Cha-ching! The nation's paper currency is designed and printed here. Guides lead 40-minute tours during which you peer down onto the work floor where millions of dollars roll off the presses and get cut (by guillotine!). It's actually a pretty dry jaunt; don't expect exciting visuals or snappy dialogue. In peak season (March to August), timed entry tickets are required. Get in line early at the **ticket kiosk** (Raoul Wallenberg Pl/15th St, South DC; ⏰from 8am Mar-Aug; 🚌Circulator National Mall, Ⓜ Orange, Silver, Blue Lines to Smithsonian). It opens at 8am. Tickets are often gone by 10am. (📞202-874-2330; www.

moneyfactory.gov; cnr 14th & C Sts SW; admission free; ⏰9-10:45am, 12:30-3:45pm & 5-6pm Mon-Fri Mar-Aug, reduced hours Sep-Feb; 🚌Circulator, Ⓜ Orange, Silver, Blue Line to Smithsonian)

Eating

Toki Underground

ASIAN $

7 ❌ MAP P88, G2

Spicy ramen noodles and dumplings sum up tiny Toki's menu. Steaming pots obscure the busy chefs, while diners slurp and sigh contentedly. The eatery takes limited reservations, so there's typically a wait. Use the opportunity to explore the surrounding bars; Toki will text when your table is ready. The restaurant isn't signposted; look for the Pug bar, and Toki is above it. (📞202-388-3086; www.tokiunderground.com; 1234 H St NE; mains $13-15; ⏰11:30am-2:30pm & 5-10pm Mon-Thu, to midnight Fri & Sat; Ⓜ Red Line to Union Station then streetcar)

Ethiopic

ETHIOPIAN $$

8 ❌ MAP P88, E2

In a city with no shortage of Ethiopian joints, Ethiopic stands above the rest thanks to its warm, stylish ambience. Top marks go to the various *wats* (stews) and the signature *tibs* (sautéed meat and veg). Vegans get lots of love too. (📞202-675-2066; www.ethiopicrestaurant.com; 401 H St NE, Capitol Hill; mains $14-20; ⏰5-10pm Tue-Thu, from noon Fri-Sun; 🥗; Ⓜ Red Line to Union Station)

Maine Avenue Fish Market

The pungent, open-air **Maine Avenue Fish Market** (www.wharfdc.com; 1100 Maine Ave SW, South DC; mains $7-13; ⏱8am-9pm; Ⓜ Orange, Silver, Blue, Yellow, Green Line to L'Enfant Plaza) is a local landmark. No-nonsense vendors sell fish, crabs, oysters and other seafood so fresh it's almost still flopping. They'll kill, strip, shell, gut, and cook your desire, which you can eat at the waterfront benches (mind the seagulls!)..

Pineapple and Pearls AMERICAN $$$

9 MAP P88, F5

Local celeb chef Aaron Silverman operates this double Michelin starred restaurant. It features a 12-course tasting menu of wild takes on comfort foods – maybe a sweetbread-stuffed chicken wing, or potato ice cream with chocolate and chestnuts. Reservations open online 10am Monday for dates five weeks in advance. (☎202-595-7375; www.pineappleandpearls.com; 715 8th St SE; tasting menu $225-325; ⏱seatings 5pm & 8pm Tue-Fri & occasional Sat; Ⓜ Orange, Silver, Blues Line to Eastern Market)

Ted's Bulletin AMERICAN $$

10 MAP P88, F5

Plop into a booth in the art-deco-meets-diner ambience, and loosen the belt. Nana's biscuits and sausage gravy for breakfast, meatloaf with ketchup glaze for dinner and other hipster spins on comfort foods hit the table. You've got to admire a place that lets you substitute pop tarts for toast. Breakfast is available all day and pulls big crowds on weekends. (☎202-544-8337; www.tedsbulletincapitolhill.com; 505 8th St SE, Capitol Hill; mains $14-24; ⏱7am-10pm Sun-Thu, to 11pm Fri & Sat; 👪; Ⓜ Orange, Silver, Blue Line to Eastern Market)

Le Grenier FRENCH $$

11 MAP P88, F2

This romantic French bistro, set in an exposed-brick row house and spread over two floors, checks all the boxes: buttery escargot, rich cheese plates, great wines, vintage Left Bank ambience. Order a sparkling aperitif, a saucy mushroom crepe or the beef bourguignon. (☎202-544-4999; www.legrenierdc.com; 502 H St NE; mains $19-27; ⏱5-10pm Tue-Thu, 5-11pm Fri, 11am-11pm Sat, 11am-10pm Sun; Ⓜ Red Line to Union Station)

Good Stuff Eatery BURGERS $

12 MAP P88, E4

Spike Mendelsohn (of *Top Chef* TV fame) is the cook behind Good Stuff, a popular burgers-shakes-and-fries spot. You can top off fries at the 'dipping bar' of various sauces, and the toasted-marshmallow milkshake comes with an honest-to-god toasted marshmallow. The ambience is that of a fast-food joint, and seats are at a premium weekend nights, when Cap Hill youth descend on the place. (📞20 2-543-8222; www.goodstuffeatery. com; 303 Pennsylvania Ave SE; burgers $7-9; ⏲11am-10pm Mon-Sat; 👪; Ⓜ Orange, Silver, Blue Line to Capitol South or Eastern Market)

Drinking

Copycat Co COCKTAIL BAR

13 🍷 MAP P88, G2

When you walk into Copycat it feels like a Chinese fast-food restaurant. That's because it is (sort of) on the 1st floor, where Chinese street-food nibbles are available. The fizzy drinks and egg-white-topped cocktails fill glasses upstairs, in the dimly lit, speakeasy-meets-opium-den-

vibed bar. Staff are unassuming and gracious in helping newbies figure out what they want from the lengthy menu. (📞202-241-1952; www.copycatcompany.com; 1110 H St NE, Capitol Hill; ⏲5pm-2am Sun-Thu, to 3am Fri & Sat; Ⓜ Red Line to Union Station then streetcar)

Bluejacket Brewery BREWERY

14 🍷 MAP P88, E6

Beer-lovers' heads will explode in Bluejacket. Pull up a stool at the mod-industrial bar, gaze at the silvery tanks bubbling up the ambitious brews, then make the hard decision about which of the 20 tap beers you want to try. A dry-hopped kolsch? Sweet-spiced stout? A cask-aged farmhouse ale? Four-ounce tasting pours

Roast duck at Pineapple and Pearls

Slave to Statesman: Frederick Douglass

Born Frederick Augustus Washington Bailey in 1818 on a slave plantation along Maryland's Eastern Shore, Frederick Douglass is remembered as one of the country's most influential and outstanding black 19th-century leaders.

In 1838, at 20 years old, he escaped wretched treatment at the hands of Maryland planters and established himself as a freeman in New Bedford, Massachusetts, eventually working for abolitionist William Lloyd Garrison's antislavery paper, the *Liberator*. After his escape, he took his new last name from a character in the Sir Walter Scott book *The Lady of the Lake*. Largely self-educated, Douglass had a natural gift for eloquence. In 1841 he won the admiration of New England abolitionists with an impromptu speech at an antislavery convention, introducing himself as 'a recent graduate from the institution of slavery,' with his 'diploma' (ie whip marks on his back).

Crusader & Underground Railroad Conductor

Douglass' effectiveness so angered proslavery forces that his supporters urged him to flee to England to escape seizure and punishment under the Fugitive Slave Law. He followed their advice and kept lecturing in England until admirers contributed enough money ($710.96) to enable him to purchase his freedom and return home in 1847.

Douglass then became the self-proclaimed station master and conductor of the Underground Railroad in Rochester, NY, working with other famed abolitionists such as Harriet Tubman and John Brown. In 1860 Douglass campaigned for Abraham Lincoln, and when the Civil War broke out, helped raise two regiments of black soldiers – the Massachusetts 54th and 55th – to fight for the Union.

Postwar Leader

After the war, Douglass went to Washington to lend his support to the 13th, 14th and 15th Constitutional Amendments, which abolished slavery, granted citizenship to former enslaved people and guaranteed citizens the right to vote.

In 1895 Douglass died at his Anacostia home, Cedar Hill, now the Frederick Douglass National Historic Site. The hilltop residence sits just across the Anacostia River, about 2 miles southeast of Nationals Park.

help with decision-making. (📞20 2-524-4862; www.bluejacketdc.com; 300 Tingey St SE, South DC; 🕙11am-1am Sun-Thu, to 2am Fri & Sat; 👫👶; Ⓜ Green Line to Navy Yard-Ballpark)

Granville Moore's PUB

15 🍺 MAP P88, G2

Besides being one of DC's best places to grab *frites* and steak au poivre, Granville Moore's has an extensive Belgian-beer menu that should satisfy any fan of low-country boozing. With its raw, wooden fixtures and walls that look like they're made from daub and mud, the interior resembles a medieval barracks. The fireside setting is ideal come winter. (📞20 2-399-2546; www.granvillemoores. com; 1238 H St NE, Capitol Hill; 🕙5-10pm Mon-Thu, to 11pm Fri, 11am-11pm Sat, 11am-10pm Sun; Ⓜ Red Line to Union Station then streetcar)

Little Miss Whiskey's Golden Dollar BAR

If Alice had returned from Wonderland so traumatized by her near beheading that she needed a stiff drink, we imagine she'd pop down to Little Miss Whiskey's (see 13 🍺 Map p88 G2) She'd love the whimsical-meets-dark-nightmares decor. And she'd probably have fun with the club kids partying on the upstairs dancefloor on weekends. She'd also adore the weirdly fantastic back patio. (www.littlemisswhiskeys. com; 1104 H St NE; 🕙5pm-2am Sun-Thu, to 3am Fri & Sat; Ⓜ Red Line to Union Station then streetcar)

Bardo Brewing BEER GARDEN

16 🍺 MAP P88, D6

Sprawled by the river in the shadow of Nationals Park, Bardo feels post-apocalyptic. Silver fermentation tanks rise from the dirt, dogs lope around rusted shipping containers, and a wire fence encircles it all. It rarely feels crowded (because it's huge), and almost always is relaxed with bearded types hobnobbing over beers. The suds tend toward brawny stouts and India Pale Ales. (www.facebook. com/bardobrewing; 25 Potomac Ave SE; 🕙5pm-midnight Mon-Fri, from 1pm Sat & Sun, closed Nov-early Mar; Ⓜ Green Line to Navy Yard)

Entertainment

Nationals Park STADIUM

17 ⭐ MAP P88, D6

The major-league Washington Nationals play baseball at this spiffy stadium beside the Anacostia River. Don't miss the mid-fourth-inning 'Presidents' Race' – an odd foot race between giant-headed caricatures of George Washington, Abraham Lincoln, Thomas Jefferson and Teddy Roosevelt. Hip bars and eateries and playful green spaces surround the ballpark, and more keep coming as the area gentrifies. (📞202-675-6287; www. mlb.com/nationals; 1500 S Capitol St SE, South DC; 📶; Ⓜ Green Line to Navy Yard-Ballpark)

Explore ⊗

Downtown, Penn Quarter & Logan Circle

This area bustles day and night. Major sights include the National Archives, where the Declaration of Independence is enshrined; the Reynolds Center for American Art & Portraiture, and Ford's Theatre, where Abraham Lincoln was assassinated. Trendy bars and restaurants proliferate, especially around Logan Circle.

The Short List

o **National Archives (p98)** Gawping at the Declaration of Independence, Constitution and Bill of Rights – the original founding documents of the USA.

o **Reynolds Center for American Art & Portraiture (p100)** Browsing the world's largest collection of US art, from George Washington's official portrait to Andy Warhol's pop art.

o **Ford's Theatre (p104)** Seeing the seat where Abraham Lincoln was assassinated, and the pistol that did it.

o **National Building Museum (p104)** Viewing the magnificent interior, modeled after a Renaissance-era palace, and imagining the glamorous occasions held here.

Getting There & Away

Ⓜ All six Metro lines cross downtown, so there are several stations here. The main ones are Metro Center (where the Red, Orange, Silver and Blue Lines hub), Gallery Pl-Chinatown (where the Green, Yellow and Red Lines merge) and Mt Vernon Sq/7th St-Convention Center (on the Green, Yellow Lines).

Neighborhood Map on p102

The National Archives (p98) JOHN M. CHASE/GETTY IMAGES ©

Top Experience 📷

See the Declaration of Independence at the National Archives

You're in line with excitable school groups, thinking your time might be better spent elsewhere. Then you enter the dim rotunda and see them – the Declaration of Independence, Constitution and Bill of Rights – the USA's founding documents. The Archives has the real, yellowing, spidery-handwriting-scrawled parchments. And your jaw drops.

◉ MAP P102, D7

www.archives.gov/museum

701 Constitution Ave NW

admission free

🕙 10am-5:30pm

Ⓜ Green, Yellow Line to Archives Navy Memorial

Declaration of Independence

The star documents are laid out in chronological order from left to right in the rotunda. Don't expect to linger over any of them – guards make you keep moving. First up is the Declaration (1776), in which the 13 US colonies announce their sovereignty and rejection of British rule. It's in pretty good shape considering it has moved around so often, including evacuations to Virginia during the War of 1812 and to Fort Knox, KY, during WWII.

Constitution & Bill of Rights

Next up is the Constitution (1787), which provides a framework for the new nation's government. A clerk named Jacob Shallus set quill to parchment and penned the document's 4543 words in two days. He was paid $30. Editors in the group can try to spot the spelling error (hint: look at the list of signatories, at the word that starts with 'p' and ends with 'sylvania'). The Bill of Rights (1789) unfurls in the next display case.

Public Vaults

The Public Vaults hold George Washington's handwritten letters and Abraham Lincoln's wartime telegrams. There's a nifty piece of paperwork from Charles 'Pa' Ingalls (of *Little House on the Prairie* fame) showing his grant application for 154 acres in the Dakota Territory. You can also watch vintage D-Day reels.

Magna Carta

A 1297 version of Magna Carta is on view in the Rubenstein Gallery. It inspired America's founding fathers with its assertion of individual rights and protections against a tyrannical ruler. The Constitution's Fifth Amendment, which restricts how the government can prosecute people accused of crimes, is a direct descendant of the older document.

★ Top Tips

o In spring and summer, reserve tickets in advance on the website for $1.50 each. This lets you go through the fast-track entrance on Constitution Dr versus the general entrance where lines can be lengthy.

o Peruse the Archives Shop for top-notch souvenirs.

o To get your bearings: the rotunda and Public Vaults are on the upper level; Magna Carta and shop are on the ground level.

✕ Take a Break

Pop in to **Red Apron Butchery** (📞20 2-524-5244; www. redapronbutchery.com; 709 D St NW, Penn Quarter; mains $5-10; ⏰8:30am-8pm Mon-Fri, from 9am Sat, 9am-5pm Sun; Ⓜ Green, Yellow Line to Archives) for coffee and filling sandwiches made with local, sustainable ingredients. Indulge in cutting-edge Indian food in modernist environs at Rasika (p107), 0.3 miles from the Archives.

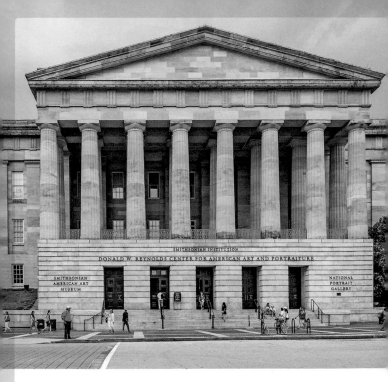

Top Experience 📷

Be Awed at the Reynolds Center for American Art & Portraiture

If you only visit one art museum in DC, make it the Reynolds Center, which combines the National Portrait Gallery and American Art Museum. There is no better collection of American art in the world than at these Smithsonian museums. It occupies three floors in the 19th-century US Patent Office building, a neoclassical beauty that hosted Lincoln's second inaugural ball.

◉ MAP P102, D6

www.americanart.si.edu

cnr 8th & F Sts NW, admission free

⊘ 11:30am-7pm

Ⓜ Red, Yellow, Green Line to Gallery Pl-Chinatown

O'Keeffe, Hopper & Folk Art

The Experience America gallery (1st floor) hangs blockbusters such as Edward Hopper's trapped woman in *Cape Cod Morning* and a slew of 1930s New Deal paintings. The nearby folk-art gallery holds a vivid collection, especially artwork by African American artists. Look for James Hampton's exquisite, foil-made throne. It's the only piece the artist ever made, a masterwork that took 14 years.

Historic Portraits

The America's Presidents gallery (2nd floor) gives due to 44 past heads of state. Gilbert Stuart's rosy-cheeked *George Washington* is the most beloved. The 'cracked plate' photo of Abraham Lincoln is also here. Then seek out *Benjamin Franklin*. You'll recognize the image, as it's the same one that now graces the $100 bill. Ben's portrait enriches the American Origins gallery (1st floor).

Modern Art

Looking for something a little more 20th-century? The 3rd floor has Andy Warhol's pop-art version of Michael Jackson and groovy paintings by David Hockney, Franz Kline, Wayne Thiebaud and more modern blue-chip artists. Nam June Paik's neon *Electric Superhighway* is so bright that it will sear your retinas.

Luce Center

The Luce Center, the museum's open storage area, spills across the 3rd and 4th floors. Wander around the trove and ogle cases of paintings. Peruse shelves stacked with sculptures, ceramics and other gorgeous objets d'art. Watch conservation artists restoring pieces in the workshop. A DIY audio tour by cell phone is available; call 202-595-1852 to begin.

★ Top Tips

o The Reynolds Center makes a good stop later in the day, given its hours of opening.

o Don't overlook the changing exhibitions. The museum curates excellent ones, including shows by big-name artists.

o Ask at any of the info desks for the *10 Highlights* brochure.

o The museum hosts loads of free public programs, including guided tours, concerts, artist talks, and sketching classes. Check the daily events calendar online.

✕ Take a Break

The museum's 1st-floor courtyard, roofed with slanting glass and dotted with olive trees and benches, is a lovely spot. Bring your own picnic or order sandwiches at the cafe (11:30am to 6:30pm; mains $9 to $13).

Matchbox Pizza (p108) beckons nearby with crisp-crust pie and craft brews.

Downtown, Penn Quarter & Logan Circle The Reynolds Center

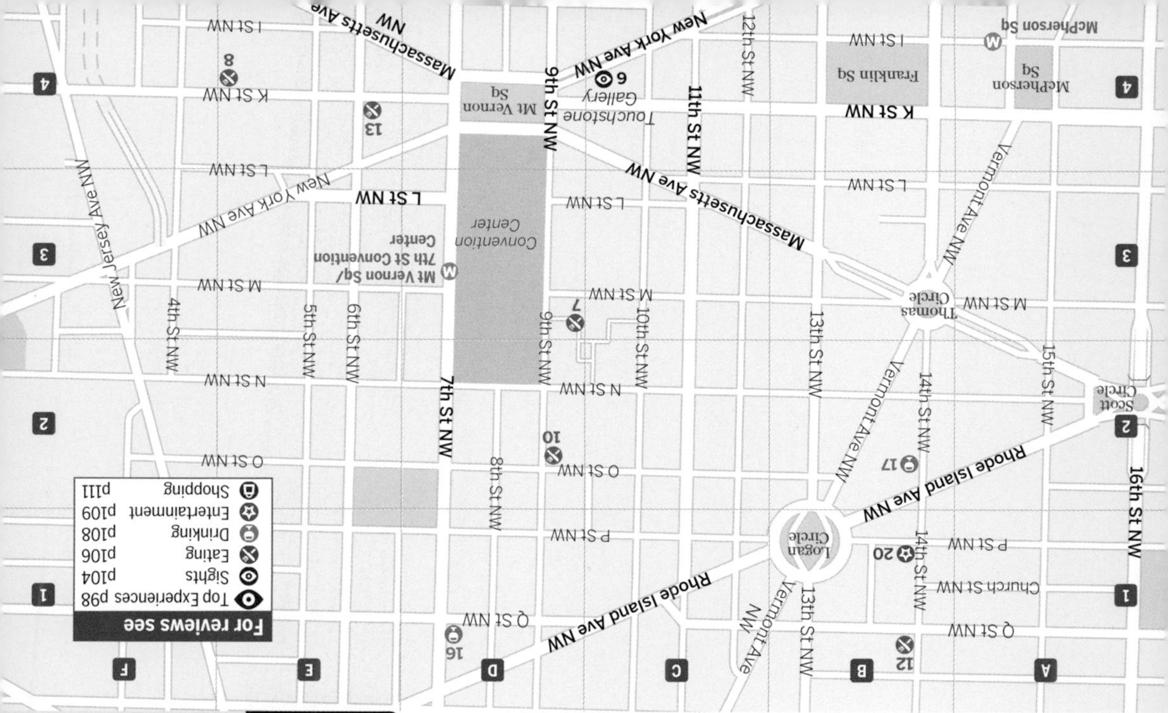

Downtown, Penn Quarter & Logan Circle

For reviews see

◉ Top Experiences p98
👁 Sights p104
✖ Eating p106
🍸 Drinking p108
★ Entertainment p109
🛍 Shopping p111

Downtown, Penn Quarter & Logan Circle

2nd St NW

North Central Fwy

3rd St NW

F St NW

4th St NW

F St NW

G St NW

● 4 National Building Museum

Ⓜ Judiciary Sq

Judiciary Sq

CHINATOWN

5th St NW

E St NW

Chinatown

Ⓜ Chinatown

● 3

6th St NW

D St NW

H St NW

John Marshall Park

4th St SW

15 ✕ 8th St NW

Capital One Arena

22 ✿

International Spy Museum

Ⓜ Gallery Place-Chinatown

7th St NW

❸ 11 ✕✕

18 19

Indiana Ave NW

E St NW

C St NW

Constitution Ave NW

Reynolds Center for American Art & Portraiture ●

PENN QUARTER

14 ✕

Ⓜ Archives

Pennsylvania Ave NW

Madison Dr NW

National Museum of Women in the Arts ● 5

23 ⓘ

11th St NW

H St NW

Ford's Theatre ● 1

10th St NW

8th St NW

9th St NW

National Archives ●

National Mall

NATIONAL MALL

DOWNTOWN

Ⓜ Metro Center

J Edgar Hoover FBI Building

F St NW

E St NW

✕ 9

10th St NW

Old Post Office Pavilion

11th St NW

12th St NW

Pennsylvania Ave NW

New York Ave NW

13th St NW

G St NW

21 ✿

Freedom Plaza

Ronald Reagan Building/International Trade Center

Federal Triangle Ⓜ

Interstate Commerce Commission

Constitution Ave NW

14th St NW

15th St NW

H St NW

Pennsylvania Ave NW

Department of Commerce Building

The Ellipse

E Executive Ave NW

15th St NW

14th St SW

0   400 m
0   0.2 miles

N

Downtown, Penn Quarter & Logan Circle

Sights

Ford's Theatre

HISTORIC SITE

1 ◎ MAP P102, C6

On April 14, 1865, John Wilkes Booth assassinated Abraham Lincoln here. Free timed-entry tickets provide access to the site, which has four parts: the theater itself (where you see the box seat Lincoln was sitting in when Booth shot him), the basement museum (displaying Booth's .44-caliber pistol, his muddy boot etc), **Petersen House** (☎202-347-4833; www.fords.org; 516 10th St NW, Penn Quarter; admission free; ☺9am-4:30pm; Ⓜ Red, Orange, Silver, Blue Line to Metro Center) (across the street, where Lincoln died) and the aftermath exhibits. Arrive early (by 8:30am) because tickets do run out. Better yet, reserve online ($3 fee) to ensure admittance. (☎202-347-4833; www.fords.org; 511 10th St NW, Penn Quarter; admission free; ☺9am-4:30pm; Ⓜ Red, Orange, Silver, Blue Line to Metro Center)

International Spy Museum

MUSEUM

2 ◎ MAP P102, D6

One of DC's most popular museums, the International Spy Museum delivers fun, interactive exhibits portraying the flashy, over-the-top world of intelligence gathering. Highlights include an immersive exhibit exploring communist Berlin, a Situation Room experience of the capture of Osama bin Laden, and an exploration of potential future cyber threats. (☎202-393-7798; www.spymuseum.org; 700 L'Enfant Plaza SW, South DC; adult/child $25/15; ☺10am-6pm Mon-Fri, 9am-7pm Sat & Sun; ⚧ Ⓜ Orange, Silver, Blue, Yellow, Green Line to L'Enfant Plaza)

Chinatown

AREA

3 ◎ MAP P102, D5

DC's dinky Chinatown is anchored on 7th and H Sts NW. It was once a major Asian American entrepôt, but today most Asian Americans in the Washington area live in the Maryland or Virginia suburbs. That said, Chinatown is still an intriguing browse. Enter through **Friendship Arch** (7th & H Sts NW, Downtown; Ⓜ Red, Yellow, Green Line to Gallery Pl-Chinatown), the largest single-span arch in the world. (7th & H Sts NW, Downtown; Ⓜ Red, Yellow, Green Line to Gallery Pl-Chinatown)

National Building Museum

MUSEUM

4 ◎ MAP P102, E6

Devoted to architecture and urban design, the museum is housed in a magnificent 1887 edifice modeled after the Renaissance-era Palazzo Farnese in Rome. The space has hosted 17 inaugural balls – from Grover Cleveland's in 1885 to Donald Trump's in 2017. It's free to view the glimmering public areas; the admission fee is for the exhibits. Step inside to see the inventive system of windows and archways that keep the Great Hall bathed in

natural light. (📞202-272-2448; www.
nbm.org; 401 F St NW, Penn Quarter;
adult/child $10/7; 🕙10am-5pm Mon-
Sat, from 11am Sun; 🚻; Ⓜ Red Line to
Judiciary Sq)

National Museum of Women in the Arts
MUSEUM

5 👁 MAP P102, B5

The only US museum exclusively
devoted to women's artwork fills
this Renaissance Revival mansion. Its collection – some 4500
works by 1000 female artists from
around the world – moves from
Renaissance artists such as Lavinia
Fontana to 20th-century works by
Frida Kahlo, Georgia O'Keeffe and
Helen Frankenthaler. Placards give
feminist interpretations of various
art movements. It's free to visit on
the first Sunday of each month.
(📞202-783-5000; www.nmwa.org;
1250 New York Ave NW, Downtown;
adult/child $10/free; 🕙10am-5pm
Mon-Sat, from noon Sun; Ⓜ Red, Orange, Silver, Blue Line to Metro Center)

Touchstone Gallery
GALLERY

6 👁 MAP P102, C4

Touchstone Gallery exhibits
contemporary pieces created by
its 45 member artists. Works cover
multiple media, including sculpture, painting and the occasional
esoteric installation. The bright,
welcoming space always has something innovative going on. (📞20
2-347-2787; www.touchstonegallery.
com; 901 New York Ave NW, Downtown;
admission free; 🕙11am-6pm Wed-Fri,
noon-5pm Sat & Sun; Ⓜ Red, Orange,
Silver, Blue Line to Metro Center)

Chinatown

KIT LEONG/SHUTTERSTOCK ©

Eating

Dabney
AMERICAN $$$

7 MAP P102, D3

Chef Jeremiah Langhorne studied historic cookbooks, discovering recipes that used local ingredients and lesser-explored flavors in his quest to resuscitate mid-Atlantic cuisine lost to the ages. Most of the dishes are even cooked over a wood-burning hearth, as in George Washington's time. Langhorne gives it all a modern twist – enough to earn him a Michelin star. (☎202-450-1015; www.thedabney. com; 122 Blagden Alley NW, Downtown; small plates $14-25; ☺5:30-10pm Tue-Thu, 5-11pm Fri & Sat, 5-10pm Sun; ⓜGreen, Yellow Line to Mt Vernon Sq/7th St-Convention Center)

A Baked Joint
CAFE $

8 MAP P102, E4

Order at the counter then take your luscious, heaped-on-house-made-bread sandwich – perhaps the smoked salmon and scallion cream cheese on an open-faced baguette, or the fried green tomatoes on buttered griddled sourdough – to a bench or table in the big, open room. Natural light streams in the floor-to-ceiling windows. (☎202-408-6985; www.abakedjoint.com; 440 K St NW, Downtown; mains $5-11; ☺7am-6pm Mon-Wed, to 10pm Thu & Fri, 8am-6pm Sat & Sun; ⓜRed, Yellow, Green Line to Gallery Pl-Chinatown)

Central Michel Richard
AMERICAN $$$

9 MAP P102, C7

Michel Richard was one of Washington's first star chefs. He died in 2016, but his namesake Central blazes on. It's a special dining experience, eating in a four-star bistro where the food is old-school, comfort-food favorites with a twist: perhaps ahi tuna burgers, a sinfully complex meatloaf, or reinvented fried chicken. (☎202-626-0015; www.centralmichelrichard.com; 1001 Pennsylvania Ave NW, Penn Quarter; mains $24-32; ☺11:30am-2:30pm Mon-Fri, 5-10pm Mon-Thu, to 10:30pm Fri & Sat, 11am-2:30pm Sun; ⓜOrange, Silver, Blue Line to Federal Triangle)

Chercher
ETHIOPIAN $

10 MAP P102, D2

Ethiopian expats have been known to compare Chercher's food to their grandma's home cooking. It prepares terrific *injera* (spongy bread) for dipping into hot spiced *wats* (stews). Vegetarians will find lots to devour. There's beer and honey wine from the motherland, and spices you can buy to go. The restaurant spreads over two floors in an intimate townhouse with brightly painted walls and artwork. (☎202-299-9703; www.chercher-restaurant.com; 1334 9th St NW; mains $11-17; ☺11am-11pm Mon-Sat, noon-10pm Sun; ☑; ⓜGreen, Yellow Line to Mt Vernon Sq/7th St-Convention Center)

Rasika

INDIAN $$

11 MAP P102, D7

Rasika is as cutting edge as Indian food gets. The room resembles a Jaipur palace decorated by modernist art-gallery curators. Top marks go to the *murgh mussalam*, a plate of juicy tandoori chicken with cashews and quail eggs; and the deceptively simple *dal* (lentils), with just the right kiss of sharp fenugreek. Vegetarians will feel a lot of love here. (202-637-1222; www.rasikarestaurant.com; 633 D St NW, Penn Quarter; mains $19-28; 11:30am-2:30pm Mon-Fri, 5:30-10:30pm Mon-Thu, 5-11pm Fri & Sat; M Green, Yellow Line to Archives-Navy Memorial-Penn Quarter)

Le Diplomate

FRENCH $$$

12 MAP P102, B1

This charming French bistro is one of the hottest tables in town. DC celebrities galore cozy up in the leather banquettes and at the sidewalk tables. They come for an authentic slice of Paris, from the coq au vin and aromatic baguettes to the vintage curios and nudie photos decorating the bathrooms. Make reservations. (202-332-3333; www.lediplomatedc.com; 1601 14th St NW, Logan Circle; mains $20-35; 5-11pm Mon-Thu, to midnight Fri, 9:30am-midnight Sat, 9:30am-11pm Sun; M Green, Yellow Line to U Street/African-American Civil War Memorial/Cardozo)

Shouk

ISRAELI $

13 MAP P102, E4

Fast and casual, Shouk creates big flavor in its vegan menu of Israeli street food, served with craft beer and tap wines. A crazy-good burger made of chickpeas, black beans, lentils and mushrooms gets stuffed into a toasty pita with pickled turnips, arugula and charred onions.

The mushroom-and-cauliflower pita and sweet-potato fries with cashew *labneh* (creamy 'cheese') are lip smacking. (202-652-1464; www.shouk.com; 655 K St NW, Downtown; mains $10; 11am-10pm; M Green, Yellow Line to Mt Vernon Sq/7th St-Convention Center)

Zaytinya

MEDITERRANEAN $$

14 MAP P102, D5

One of the culinary crown jewels of chef José Andrés, ever-popular Zaytinya serves superb Greek, Turkish and Lebanese meze in a long, noisy dining room with soaring ceilings and all-glass walls.

It's a favorite after-work meet-up spot for wine, cocktails, and a nibble. (202-638-0800; www.zaytinya.com; 701 9th St NW, Penn Quarter; meze $8-14; 11am-10pm Mon & Sun, to 11pm Tue-Thu, to midnight Fri & Sat; M Red, Yellow, Green Line to Gallery Pl-Chinatown)

El Sol

This restaurant (☎202-815-4789; www.elsol-dc.com; 1227 11th St NW, Downtown; tacos $3-3.50, mains $10-16; ☺10am-1am Sun-Thu, to 2am Fri & Sat; ⓜGreen, Yellow Line to Mt Vernon Sq/7th St-Convention Center) feels like a sunny neighborhood taqueria, but the food goes way beyond. Thin, crisp corn tortillas cradle juicy chicken, slow-braised pork, cactus paddles and more, with almost all ingredients made in house (the mole sauce comes from the chef's mom in Mexico).

Matchbox Vintage Pizza Bistro

PIZZA $

15 ⓧ MAP P102, D5

The pizza here has a devout following of gastronomes and the restaurant's warm, exposed-brick interior is typically packed. What's so good about it? Fresh ingredients, a thin, blistered crust baked by angels, and more fresh ingredients. Oh, and the beer list rocks, with Belgian ales and hopped-up craft brews flowing from the taps. Reserve ahead to avoid a wait. (☎202-289-4441; www.matchbox restaurants.com; 713 H St NW, Downtown; 10in pizzas $13-20; ☺11am-10:30pm Mon-Thu, to 11:30pm Fri, 10am-11:30pm Sat, 10am-10:30pm Sun; ⓜRed, Yellow, Green Line to Gallery Pl-Chinatown)

Drinking

Dacha Beer Garden   BEER GARDEN

16 ⓔ MAP P102, D1

Happiness reigns in Dacha's freewheeling beer garden. Kids and dogs bound around the picnic tables, while adults hoist glass boots filled with German brews. When the weather gets nippy, staff bring blankets and stoke the firepit. (☎202-350-9888; www.dachadc.com; 1600 7th St NW, Shaw; ☺4-10:30pm Mon, Tue & Thu, 3pm-midnight Fri, 8am-midnight Sat, noon-10:30pm Sun, reduced hours winter; ♿♠; ⓜGreen, Yellow Line to Shaw-Howard U)

Churchkey   BAR

17 ⓔ MAP P102, B2

Coppery, mod-industrial Churchkey glows with hipness. Fifty beers flow from the taps, plus five brain-walloping, cask-aged ales. If none of those please you, another 500 types of brew are available by bottle (including gluten-free suds). Churchkey is the upstairs counterpart to **Birch & Barley** (☎202-567-2576; www.birchandbarley.com; 1337 14th St NW, Logan Circle; mains $17-29; ☺5:30-10pm Tue-Thu, to 11pm Fri, 11am-3pm & 5:30-11pm Sat, 11am-3pm & 5-9pm Sun; ⓜOrange, Silver, Blue Line to McPherson Sq), a popular nouveau comfort-food restaurant, and you can order much of its menu at the bar. (☎202-567-2576; www.churchkeydc.com; 1337 14th St NW, Logan Circle; ☺4pm-1am Mon-Thu, to

2am Fri, 11:30am–2am Sat, 11:30am–1am Sun; Orange, Silver, Blue Line to McPherson Sq)

Entertainment

Shakespeare Theatre Company
THEATER

18 ⭐ MAP P102, D6

The nation's foremost Shakespeare company presents masterful works by the Bard, as well as plays by George Bernard Shaw, Oscar Wilde, Eugene O'Neill and others.

The season spans about a half-dozen productions annually, plus a free summer Shakespeare series for two weeks in late August. (☏20 2-547-1122; www.shakespearetheatre.org; 450 7th St NW, Lansburgh Theatre, Penn Quarter; average ticket $85; Ⓜ Green, Yellow Line to Archives-Navy Memorial-Penn Quarter)

Woolly Mammoth Theatre Company
THEATER

19 ⭐ MAP P102, D7

Set up in DC in 1978, Woolly Mammoth is the edgiest of the city's experimental theatre groups. For most shows, $20 'stampede' seats are available two hours before performances.

They're limited in number, and sold first-come, first-served. (☏20 2-393-3939; www.woollymammoth.net; 641 D St NW, Penn Quarter; average ticket $67; Ⓜ Green, Yellow Line to Archives-Navy Memorial-Penn Quarter)

Matchbox Vintage Pizza Bistro

TOPPHOTOIMAGES/GETTY IMAGES ©

Downtown, Penn Quarter & Logan Circle Entertainment

Tragedy at Ford's Theatre

A Murderous Plan

In 1865, just days after the Confederate Army surrendered, President Abraham Lincoln was gunned down in cold blood.

John Wilkes Booth – Marylander, famous actor and die-hard believer in the Confederate cause – had long harbored ambitions to bring the US leadership to its knees. On April 14, when he stopped by Ford's Theatre to retrieve his mail, he learned the president would be attending a play that evening. Booth decided it was time to strike.

He met with his co-conspirators and hatched a plan: Lewis Powell would kill Secretary of State William Seward at his home, while George Atzerodt killed Vice President Andrew Johnson at his residence and Booth struck Lincoln – all would happen simultaneously around 10pm. As it turns out, only Booth would succeed in his mission.

Assassination & Getaway

That night, as Booth strolled up to Lincoln's box, no one questioned him, as he was a well-known actor at Ford's. He crept inside and barricaded the outer door behind him (Lincoln's bodyguard had headed to a nearby pub at intermission and never returned). Booth knew the play well, and waited until he heard the funniest line of the play '... you sockdologizing old man-trap!' before he struck. As the audience predictably erupted in laughter, Booth crept behind Lincoln and shot him in the head.

The president's lifeless body slumped forward. Mary Lincoln screamed and Major Henry Rathbone, also in Lincoln's box, tried to seize the assassin. Booth stabbed him then leaped onto the stage. His foot, however, became entangled in the flag decorating the box, and he landed badly, fracturing his leg. He stumbled to his feet and held the bloody dagger aloft, saying *Sic semper tyrannis!* ('Thus to all tyrants!'). Booth fled the theater, mounted his waiting horse and galloped off to meet his co-conspirators.

Death Toll

Lincoln never regained consciousness. He was carried across the street to the Petersen House, where he died early the next morning. In a massive manhunt, Booth was hunted down and shot to death less than two weeks later. His alleged co-conspirators were also discovered, brought to trial and executed on July 7.

Studio Theatre THEATER

20 ⭐ MAP P102, B1

This modern four-theater complex has been staging Pulitzer Prize–winning and premiere plays for more than 35 years. It cultivates a lot of local actors. Discounted 'rush' tickets ($30) are sometimes available 30 minutes before showtime (☎202-332-3300; www.studiotheatre.org; 1501 14th St NW; tickets from $45; Ⓜ Red Line to Dupont Circle)

National Theatre THEATER

21 ⭐ MAP P102, B6

Washington's oldest continuously operating theater shows flashy Broadway musicals and big-name productions. A lottery for $25 tickets (cash only) takes place two hours prior to every show; submit your name at the box office. Saturday mornings feature free performances for children at 9:30am and 11am; it's best to reserve tickets online in advance. (☎202-628-6161; www.thenationaldc.org; 1321 Pennsylvania Ave NW, Penn Quarter; averageg ticket $65; Ⓜ Red, Orange, Silver, Blue Line to Metro Center)

Capital One Arena STADIUM

22 ⭐ MAP P102, D6

This ever-busy facility is DC's arena for big-name concerts and sporting events. Washington's rough-and-tumble pro-hockey team the Capitals and pro-basketball team the Wizards both play here from October through April.

The women's pro basketball team the Mystics take over from May through August. (☎20 2-628-3200; https://capitalonearena. monumentalsportsnetwork.com; 601 F St NW, Penn Quarter; tickets from $40; Ⓜ Red, Yellow, Green Line to Gallery Pl-Chinatown)

Shopping

CityCenterDC SHOPPING CENTER

23 🔒 MAP P102, C5

Rodeo Drive chic may not be the first way you'd think of describing Washington, but this sparkling, open-air oasis of shops and restaurants blows that notion straight out of the water.

Style mavens peruse high-end boutiques, while diners indulge in haute cuisine. (☎202-289-9000; www.citycenterdc.com; H St NW, between 9th & 11th Sts NW, Downtown; Ⓜ Red, Orange, Silver, Blue Line to Metro Center, Red, Yellow, Green Line to Gallery Pl-Chinatown)

Walking Tour 🚶

Exploring Jazzy U Street & Shaw

In the early 1900s, U St was one of the most vibrant African American districts in the country. Duke Ellington was born here and cut his chops in local clubs. Today U St and Shaw (the surrounding area) are DC's 'it' spots. Poetry slams, soul food and, of course, Duke's old jazz hangouts make it a sweet slice of DC life.

Start Busboys & Poets

Finish Howard Theatre

Length 1 mile

Metro Green or Yellow Line to U St (for places around U St and 13th St NW) and Shaw-Howard U (for places around T St and 7th St NW).

❶ Open Mike at Busboys & Poets

Busboys & Poets (www.busboy-sandpoets.com; 2021 14th St NW, U Street; mains $16-22; ⏲7am-midnight Mon-Thu, to 1am Fri, 8am-1am Sat, 8am-midnight Sun; 🛜🎤) is one of U St's linchpins. The big event is the open-mike poetry reading every Tuesday from 9pm to 11pm.

❷ Half-Smokes at Ben's Chili Bowl

Despite visits by presidents, movie stars and busloads of tourists, **Ben's Chili Bowl** (www.benschili bowl.com; 1213 U St NW, U Street; mains $6-10; ⏲6am-2am Mon-Thu, to 4am Fri, 7am-4am Sat, 11am-midnight Sun) remains a real neighborhood spot, with locals downing half-smokes (a smokier version of the hotdog) and gossiping over sweet iced tea.

❸ Tunes at U Street Music Hall

Two local DJs own and operate **U Street Music Hall** (www.ustreet-musichall.com; 1115 U St NW, U Street; tickets $10-25; ⏲hours vary;). It looks like a no-frills rock bar, but it has a pro sound system, cork-cushioned dance floor and other accoutrements of a serious dance club.

❹ Soul Food at Oohh's & Aahh's

Un-notch the belt: the cornbread, collard greens, meatloaf and other soulfood dishes at **Oohh's & Aahh's** (www.oohhsnaahhs.com; 1005 U St NW; mains $14-22; ⏲noon-10pm Mon-Thu, to 4am Fri & Sat, to 7pm Sun) come in enormous portions.

❺ Art at Foundry Gallery

A nonprofit member-run organization, **Foundry Gallery** (www.foundrygallery.org; 2118 8th St NW; admission free; ⏲1-7pm Wed-Sun) features a diverse range of super-contemporary art all created by local artists.

❻ Beer at Right Proper

As if the artwork – a mural of the National Zoo's giant pandas with laser eyes destroying DC – wasn't enough, **Right Proper Brewing Co** (www.rightproperbrewery.com; 624 T St NW, Logan Circle; ⏲5-11pm Mon-Thu, 11:30am-midnight Fri & Sat, 11:30am-10pm Sun) makes sublime ales where Duke Ellington played pool.

❼ Big Names at Howard Theatre

Built in 1910, **Howard Theatre** (www.thehowardtheatre.com; 620 T St NW, U Street; tickets from $27) was the top address when U St was known as 'Black Broadway.' Ellington, Ella Fitzgerald, Billie Holiday and more lit the marquee. Now big-name comedians, blues and jazz acts fill the house.

Explore ◈
Dupont Circle

*Dupont offers flashy new restaurants, hip bars, cafe
society and cool bookstores. The neighborhood has
Washington's highest concentration of embassies,
many in historic mansions. It's also the heart of the
LGBTIQ+ community.*

The Short List

○ **Embassy Row (p120)** *Searching for Tunisia, Chile,
Turkmenistan, Togo, Haiti – flags flutter above heavy
doors and mark the nations inside.*

○ **Phillips Collection (p120)** *Getting up close to Re-
noirs, Gauguins and Picassos in a restored mansion.*

○ **Kramerbooks (p117)** *Browsing the stacks in the big,
sunny store, then heading into the cafe to sip cocktails
and stuff your face.*

○ **National Geographic Museum (p120)** *Visiting the
headquarters of the famed explorers' society to see
artifacts from their expeditions.*

○ **Woodrow Wilson House** *(www.woodrowwilsonhouse.
org; 2340 S St NW; adult/child $10/free; ⊙10am-4pm
Wed-Sun Mar-Dec, Fri-Sun only Jan & Feb; MRed Line to
Dupont Circle) Experiencing the genteel Washingtonian
lifestyle, past and present.*

Getting There & Away

M Dupont Circle (Red Line) for most points. Use the Q St exit
for destinations north of P St, and the 19th St exit for destinations south. Farragut North (Red Line) is closer to M St.

🚌 Catch the DC Circulator's Dupont–Georgetown–Rosslyn
bus at 19th and N Sts (use the south exit from Dupont Metro
Station).

Neighborhood Map on p118

Kramerbooks, Dupont Circle (p117)

Walking Tour 🥾

A Night Out in Dupont Circle

Dupont gets busy once the sun goes down. Young professionals of all stripes and persuasions gather with friends to drink, dine and sing karaoke. They play board games, quaff sparkling wines, indulge in late-night gelati and burgers, and flirt with each other in the 3am bookshop on weekends.

Start Bistrot du Coin
Finish Tabard Inn Bar
Length 1 mile
Metro Red Line to Dupont Circle

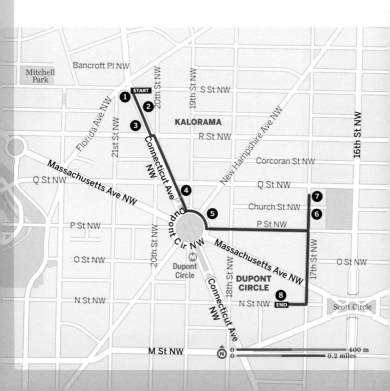

❶ Wine at Bistrot du Coin

Lively and much-loved **Bistrot du Coin** (www.bistrotducoin.com; 1738 Connecticut Ave NW, Dupont Circle; mains $20-30; ⏱11:30am-midnight Mon-Wed, 11:30am-1am Thu & Fri, noon-1am Sat, noon-midnight Sun) is a neighborhood favorite for roll-up-your sleeves, working-class French fare. If it's busy, try for a bar seat.

❷ Board Room's Games

Order a pitcher of beer and prepare to outwit your opponent at Battleship. Or unleash your tic-tac-toe skills with Connect 4. **Board Room** (www.boardroomdc.com; 1737 Connecticut Ave NW, Dupont Circle; ⏱4pm-2am Mon-Thu, 4pm-3am Fri, noon-3am Sat, noon-2am Sun) has all of your favorite childhood games.

❸ Gelato at Dolcezza

Dolcezza (www.dolcezzagelato.com; 1704 Connecticut Ave NW, Dupont Circle; gelato $6-8; ⏱7am-10pm Mon-Thu, 7am-11pm Fri, 8am-11pm Sat, 8am-10pm Sun; 🛜) scoops a dozen or so creamy flavors of gelati. They're not your everyday spoonful, with varieties such as lemon ricotta cardamom and strawberry tarragon.

❹ Late-Night Books

Open almost round the clock on weekends, **Kramerbooks** (www.kramers.com; 1517 Connecticut Ave NW, Dupont Circle; ⏱7:30am-1am Sun-Thu, to 3am Fri & Sat) is as much a spot for schmoozing as for shopping. Grab a meal, have a pint and flirt with comely strangers (the store is a fabled pick-up spot).

❺ Underground Art

Who knew there was a forsaken streetcar station sprawled beneath Dupont Circle? A local arts group revamped it into **Dupont Underground** (www.dupontunderground.org; 1583 New Hampshire Ave NW; from $15), a cavernous gallery of art, architecture and design.

❻ Curry at Duke's Grocery

Duke's Grocery (www.dukesgrocery.com; 1513 17th St NW; mains $12-16; ⏱11am-10pm Mon & Tue, 11am-1am Wed & Thu, 11am-2am Fri, 10am-2am Sat, 10am-10pm Sun; 🛜) takes its cue from East London's corner cafes and pubs. A chalkboard lists the daily-changing menu.

❼ Karaoke at JR's

Gay hangout **JR's** (www.jrsbar-dc.com; 1519 17th St NW, Dupont Circle; ⏱4pm-2am Mon-Thu, 4pm-3am Fri, 1pm-3am Sat, 1pm-2am Sun) is usually packed. While it's mostly guys under 40 in natty-casual attire chatting over their beers, the dark-wood and stained-glass bar is welcoming to all.

❽ Tabard Inn Cocktails

It may be in a hotel, but lots of locals pile into the **Tabard Inn Bar** (www.tabardinn.com; 1739 N St NW; ⏱11:30am-11pm;) to linger over a brandy or an old-fashioned.

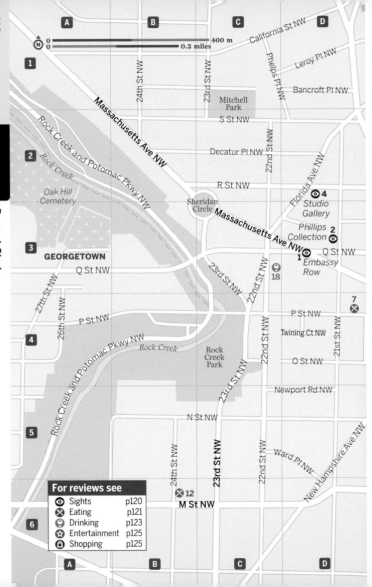

California St NW

Leroy Pl NW

Bancroft Pl NW

A · B · C · D

1

0 — 400 m
0 — 0.2 miles

24th St NW

23rd St NW

Phelps Pl NW

Massachusetts Ave NW

Mitchell Park

S St NW

2

Rock Creek and Potomac Pkwy NW

Rock Creek

Oak Hill Cemetery

Decatur Pl NW

R St NW

22nd St NW

Florida Ave NW

4 Studio Gallery

Phillips Collection **2**

3

GEORGETOWN

Q St NW

Sheridan Circle

Massachusetts Ave NW

23rd St NW

22nd St NW

1 Embassy Row

Q St NW

🍴 18

27th St NW

26th St NW

P St NW

21st St NW

7 ✕

4

Rock Creek and Potomac Pkwy NW

Rock Creek

Rock Creek Park

23rd St NW

22nd St NW

P St NW

Twining Ct NW

O St NW

Newport Rd NW

5

N St NW

24th St NW

23rd St NW

22nd St NW

Ward Pl NW

New Hampshire Ave NW

6

12 ✕

M St NW

For reviews see

◎	Sights	p120
✕	Eating	p121
🍴	Drinking	p123
☆	Entertainment	p125
🛍	Shopping	p125

Sights

Embassy Row
ARCHITECTURE

1 ⊙ MAP P118, D3

Want to take a trip around the world? Stroll northwest along Massachusetts Ave from Dupont Circle (the actual traffic circle) and you pass more than 40 embassies housed in mansions that range from elegant to imposing to discreet. Tunisia, Chile, Turkmenistan, Togo, Haiti – flags flutter above heavy doors and mark the nations inside, while dark-windowed sedans ease out of driveways ferrying diplomats to and fro. The district has another 130 embassies sprinkled throughout, but this is the main vein. (www.embassy.org; Massachusetts Ave NW, btwn Observatory & Dupont Circles NW, Dupont Circle; M Red Line to Dupont Circle)

Phillips Collection
MUSEUM

2 ⊙ MAP P118, D3

The country's first modern-art museum (opened in 1921) houses a small but exquisite collection of European and American works. Renoir's *Luncheon of the Boating Party* is a highlight, along with pieces by Gauguin, Van Gogh, Matisse, Picasso and many other greats. The intimate rooms, set in a restored mansion and adjacent former apartment building, put you unusually close to the artworks. Download the free app or dial 202-595-1839 for audio tours through the works. (📞202-387-2151; www.phillipscollection.org; 1600 21st St NW, Dupont Circle; Tue-Fri free, Sat & Sun $10, ticketed exhibitions $12; ⌚10am-5pm Tue, Wed, Fri & Sat, to 8:30pm Thu, noon-6:30pm Sun; 🚌Circulator Dupont Circle-Georgetown-Rosslyn, M Red Line to Dupont Circle)

National Geographic Museum
MUSEUM

3 ⊙ MAP P118, G6

The museum at National Geographic Society headquarters can't compete with the Smithsonian's more extensive offerings, but it can be worth a stop, depending on what's showing. Exhibits are drawn from the society's well-documented expeditions to the far corners of the earth, and they change periodically. (📞202-857-7700; www.nationalgeographic.org/dc; 1145 17th St NW, Dupont Circle; adult/child $15/10; ⌚10am-6pm; M Red Line to Farragut North)

Studio Gallery
GALLERY

4 ⊙ MAP P118, D2

Studio Gallery shows contemporary works by more than 35 emerging DC-area artists. Paintings, sculpture, mixed media and video are represented. The relatively small space spans the main floor and basement, with exhibits that always feel fresh. Openings are held on the first Friday of the month. (📞202-232-8734; www.studiogallerydc.com; 2108 R St NW; admission free; ⌚1-6pm Wed-Fri, from 11am Sat; M Red Line to Dupont Circle)

Eating

Little Serow THAI $$$

5  MAP P118, G4

Set in a cavern-like green basement, Little Serow has no phone, reservations or outside signage, and it only seats groups of four or fewer. Despite this, people line up around the block for superlative northern Thai cuisine. The menu, changes weekly. (www.littleserow. com; 1511 17th St NW, Dupont Circle; prix-fixe menu $54; ⊕5:30-10pm Tue-Thu, to 10:30pm Fri & Sat; ⓂRed Line to Dupont Circle)

Bub & Pop's SANDWICHES $

6  MAP P118, F6

A chef tired of the fine-dining rat race opened this gourmet sandwich shop with his parents. Ingredients are made in-house from scratch – the meatballs, pickles, mayonnaise and roasted pork. Congenial mom Arlene rules the counter and can answer questions about any of it. The sandwiches are enormous, and best consumed hot off the press. (☎202-457-1111; www.bubandpops.com; 1815 M St NW, Dupont Circle; sandwiches half/whole $10/18; ⊕8am-7pm Mon-Fri, 11am-4pm Sat; ⓂRed Line to Dupont Circle)

Obelisk ITALIAN $$$

7  MAP P118, D4

Obelisk's small and narrow dining room feels almost like eating at someone's kitchen table. The set-course Italian feasts are prepared with first-rate ingredients. You might sup on ricotta ravioli with

The National Geographic Museum

KRISTI BLOKHIN/SHUTTERSTOCK ©

green tomato sauce, or braised duck leg with pear sauce; the antipasti in particular is a revelation. The menu changes daily but doesn't give you much selection (picky eaters should call ahead). Make reservations. (☎202-872-1180; www.obeliskdc.com; 2029 P St NW; 5-course menu $78-88; ☕6-10pm Tue-Sat; Ⓜ Red Line to Dupont Circle)

Un Je Ne Sais Quoi

BAKERY $

8 ✗ MAP P118, F4

The smell of rich coffee envelops you when you enter this little bakery, where a couple of French expats bake *merveilleux*, their signature pastry plumped with layers of meringue and ganache. It's like biting into a glorious cloud. Tarts, eclairs and other sweets are equally exquisite, served on china plates amid vintage Parisian decor.

(☎202-721-0099; www.facebook. com/unjenesaisquoipastry; 1361 Connecticut Ave NW; pastries $2.50-5; ☕7:30am-7pm Mon-Thu, 7:30am-8pm Fri, 10am-8pm Sat; Ⓜ Red Line to Dupont Circle)

Zorba's Cafe

GREEK $

9 ✗ MAP P118, E3

Generous portions of moussaka and souvlaki, as well as pitchers of Rolling Rock beer, make family-run Zorba's Cafe one of DC's best bargain haunts. On warm days the outdoor patio packs with locals. With the bouzouki music playing in the background, you can almost imagine you're in the Greek islands. (☎202-387-8555; www.zorbas cafe.com; 1612 20th St NW, Dupont Circle; mains $13-15; ☕11am-11:30pm Mon-Sat, to 10:30pm Sun; 🚹; Ⓜ Red Line to Dupont Circle)

Scallops, Blue Duck Tavern

/GETTY IMAGES ©

St Arnold's Mussel Bar

BELGIAN $$

10 MAP P118, F5

Mussels and *frites* (fries) hit the tables in innumerable varieties: in Thai curry sauce, bleu cheese and bacon sauce, and the house specialty beer sauce with caramelized shallots and duck fat, to name a few. Add the terrific Belgian beers on tap and the warm, convivial ambience, and it's easy to settle in for a while. (☏ 202-833-1321; www. starnoldsmusselbar.com; 1827 Jefferson Pl NW; mains $14-20; ☺ 11am-2am Sun-Thu, to 3am Fri & Sat; Ⓜ Red Line to Farragut North)

Hank's Oyster Bar

SEAFOOD $$$

11 MAP P118, H3

DC has several oyster bars, but mini-chain Hank's is our favorite, mixing power-player muscle with a casual, beachy ambience. As you'd expect, the oyster menu is extensive and excellent; there are always at least four varieties on hand, along with lobster rolls, fried clams and witty cocktails. It's best to reserve ahead. (☏ 202-462-4265; www.hanksoysterbar.com; 1624 Q St NW, Dupont Circle; mains $28-36; ☺ 11:30am-1am Mon-Thu, 11:30am-2am Fri, 11am-2am Sat, 11am-1am Sun; Ⓜ Red Line to Dupont Circle)

Blue Duck Tavern

AMERICAN $$$

12 MAP P118, B5

A reliable rave winner, the Michelin-starred Blue Duck creates a rustic kitchen ambience in

Larry's Lounge

An agreeably worn neighborhood joint, **Larry's Lounge** (☏ 202-483-1483; 1840 18th St NW; ☺ 4pm-2am Mon-Thu, to 3am Fri & Sat, 2pm-2am Sun; 🐾; Ⓜ Red Line to Dupont Circle) is known for its potently boozy drinks, dog-friendly patio and big windows prime for people-watching. It's a gay bar, but plenty of straight patrons settle in to take advantage of its virtues. Prepare for a chat with a cast of characters.

the midst of an uber-urbanized corridor of M St. The changing menu draws from farms across the country, mixing mains such as venison tartare and suckling pig sourced from Pennsylvania, crab cakes from nearby Chesapeake Bay and grits from Virginia. Weekend brunch is a big to-do. (☏ 202-419-6755; www.blueducktavern. com; 1201 24th St NW; mains $30-46; ☺ 6:30am-2:30pm & 5:30-10:30pm Sun-Thu, to 11pm Fri & Sat, 🥢; Ⓜ Red Line to Dupont Circle)

Drinking

Bar Charley

BAR

13 🚇 MAP P118, F1

Bar Charley draws a mixed crowd from the neighborhood – young, old, gay and straight. They come for groovy cocktails sloshing in vintage glassware and ceramic tiki mugs, served at very reasonable prices by DC standards. Try the gin and gingery Suffering Bastard. The beer list isn't huge, but it's thoughtfully chosen with some wild ales. Around 60 wines available too. (📞202-627-2183; www.barcharley.com; 1825 18th St NW, Dupont Circle; ⊙5pm-12:30am Mon-Thu, 4pm-1:30am Fri, 10am-1:30am Sat, 10am-midnight Sun; Ⓜ Red Line to Dupont Circle)

18th Street Lounge CLUB

14 🍸 MAP P118, F5

Chandeliers, velvet sofas, antique wallpaper and a ridiculously good-looking, dance-loving crowd adorn this multifloored mansion. The DJs – spinning funk, soul and house – are phenomenal, which is not surprising given Eric Hilton (of Thievery Corporation) is co-owner. The lack of a sign on the door proclaims the club's exclusivity. No athletic attire or sneakers. Cover charge ranges from $10 to $20. (📞202-466-3922; www.eighteenthstreetlounge.com; 1212 18th St NW; ⊙5pm-2am Tue-Thu, 5pm-3am Fri, 9pm-3am Sat, 9pm-2am Sun; Ⓜ Red Line to Dupont Circle)

Filter CAFE

15 🍸 MAP P118, E2

Set on a quiet street, Filter is a jewel-box-sized cafe with a tiny front patio, a hipster crowd, sullen baristas and, most importantly, good, locally roasted coffee.

You can get a dandy flat white here. (📞202-234-5837; www.filter

coffeehouse.com; 1726 20th St NW; ⊙7am-7pm Mon-Fri, 8am-7pm Sat & Sun; Ⓜ Red Line to Dupont Circle)

Firefly Bar BAR

16 🍸 MAP P118, E5

Firefly is a restaurant first – the Hotel Madera's restaurant, to be precise – but we're not listing it for those merits. We can say it's one of the coolest bars in Dupont, decked out with its surreal, magically happy 'firefly trees,' all candlelit and reminiscent of childhood summer evenings, and romantic as hell to boot. The cocktail menu is a glorious thing. (📞202-861-1310; www.firefly-dc.com; 1310 New Hampshire Ave NW; ⊙4-11pm; Ⓜ Red Line to Dupont Circle)

Decades CLUB

17 🍸 MAP P118, F5

Decades is a big, booming club with three levels of let-loose dance music: one each for '80s, '90s and 2000s jams. It's good fun, decorated with glowy retro decor and arcade games. No sneakers or athletic gear allowed. There's a $20 cover charge most days. (📞202-853-3498; www.decadesdc.com; 1219 Connecticut Ave NW; ⊙9pm-2am Thu, to 3am Fri & Sat; Ⓜ Red Line to Dupont Circle)

Bier Baron Tavern BAR

18 🍸 MAP P118, C3

Enter the Bier Baron's underground lair and prepare your liver for an onslaught of brews. The dark, dingy, pubby bar taps 50 different beers – emphasis on local and unusual craft suds – and offers 500 more bottled beers from around the world. Aim for a corner seat, order a sampler and settle in for an impressive taste tour. (📞 202-293-1887; http://inlovewithbier.com; 1523 22nd St NW; ⏰4pm-midnight Mon-Thu, to 2am Fri & Sat, to 11pm Sun; Ⓜ️Red Line to Dupont Circle)

Entertainment

DC Improv
COMEDY

19 ⭐ MAP P118, F6

DC Improv is comedy in the traditional sense, featuring stand-up by comics from *Comedy Central*, *Saturday Night Live* and HBO in its main theater. The smaller 'lounge showroom' hosts wise-cracking, up-and-coming improv troupes, usually with cheaper ticket prices. The venue also offers workshops for those who would like to hone their laugh-getting skills. (📞 202-296-7008; www.dcimprov.com; 1140 Connecticut Ave NW; tickets $10-22; ⏰closed Mon; Ⓜ️Red Line to Farragut North)

Shopping

Second Story Books
BOOKS, MUSIC

20 🔒 MAP P118, E4

Packed with dusty secondhand tomes, atmospheric Second Story

Dupont Circle Market

The **Dupont Circle Market** (www.freshfarm.org; 1500 20th St NW; ⏰8:30am-1:30pm Sun; Ⓜ️Red Line to Dupont Circle) teems with locals on Sunday morning. It's part of the Fresh Farm Market program, one of the leaders of the Chesapeake Bay region local-food movement.

also sells used CDs (mostly jazz and classical), antiquarian books and old sheet music. The prices are decent and the choices are broad (particularly in the realm of history and Americana). (📞 202-659-8884; www.secondstorybooks. com; 2000 P St NW; ⏰10am-10pm; Ⓜ️Red Line to Dupont Circle)

Tabletop
HOMEWARES

21 🔒 MAP P118, E3

Also known as the best little design store in Dupont, Tabletop is evidence that DC is a lot more stylish than some give it credit for. The whimsical candles, postmodern wine carafes and vintage table linens are sure to impress your arty and creative friends. (📞 202-387-7117; www.tabletopdc.com; 1608 20th St NW; ⏰noon-8pm Mon-Sat, 10am-6pm Sun; Ⓜ️Red Line to Dupont Circle)

Walking Tour 🚶

Embassies & Mansions

Embassies sprinkle the District, but Dupont Circle has the most. Massachusetts Ave was once Millionaire's Row, and the mansions of the old elite are still thick on the ground. Most embassies were residences built by industrialists and financiers at the turn of the 20th century. The Great Depression caused many to lose their manors, which stood gracefully decaying until WWII's end.

Start Dupont Circle
Finish Spanish Steps
Length 1 mile; 45 minutes

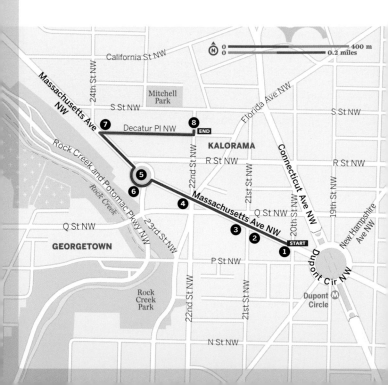

❶ Blaine Mansion

In 1881 Republican party founder 'Slippery Jim' Blaine built the haunted-house-creepy Blaine Mansion at 2000 Massachusetts Ave, now the oldest mansion in Dupont. He lived there less than two years, not because he was spooked by bizarre architecture, but because his political fortunes changed.

❷ Indonesian Embassy

The Walsh-McLeanHouse at No 2020 is now the Indonesian Embassy. Gold-mining magnate Thomas Walsh commissioned the home in 1903. He embedded in the foundation a gold nugget, which has never been found.

❸ Anderson House

Continue up Massachusetts Ave to No 2118 and the grand Anderson House, base of the Society of the Cincinnati, a group that educates the public about the Revolutionary War. It's one of the few homes you can go inside. The ballrooms, chandeliers and staircases drop the jaw.

❹ Luxembourg Embassy

The Luxembourg Embassy at No 2200 is a showstopper. Alexander Stewart built the home in 1909 in the grand court style of Louis XIV. In 1941 the Grand Duchess of Luxembourg bought it and lived there during WWII.

❺ Sheridan Circle

Soon you'll approach Sheridan Circle, centered on Gutzon Borglum's equestrian statue of Civil War General Philip Sheridan. Borglum later sculpted Mt Rushmore.

❻ Turkish Ambassador's Residence

Edward Everett, inventor of the grooved bottle cap, built what is now the Turkish Ambassador's Residence, on the corner of Sheridan Circle and 23rd St. George Oakley Totten designed the building.

❼ Croatian Embassy

At No 2343 Massachusetts Ave, a cross-legged sculpture of St Jerome dreams over his book. The masterpiece is the work of Croatian sculptor Ivan Meštrović; appropriately, it fronts the Croatian Embassy.

❽ Spanish Steps

Detour east on Decatur Pl to 22nd St. The rise up to S St NW was too steep, so city planners constructed a pedestrian staircase, dubbed the Spanish Steps for its resemblance to Rome's Piazza di Spagna. Climb up and stare across the area you've traversed.

Explore ◈

Adams Morgan

Adams Morgan has long been Washington's fun, nightlife-driven party zone. It's also a global village of sorts. The result today is a raucous mash-up centered on 18th St NW. Vintage boutiques, record shops and ethnic eats poke up between thumping bars and a growing number of stylish spots for gastronomes.

The Short List

○ **18th St NW (p130)** *Exploring where Ethiopians, Koreans, Indians, Cubans and hard drinkers collide in a row of restaurants, music clubs, dive bars, and boutiques.*

○ **Tail Up Goat (p131)** *Pretending you're on a breezy island, sharing lemony plates of ribs and sunny cocktails.*

○ **Jack Rose Dining Saloon** (☏202-588-7388; www. jackrosediningsaloon.com; 2007 18th St NW; ◷5pm-2am Sun-Thu, to 3am Fri & Sat; Ⓜ Red Line to Dupont Circle) *Ogling the largest whiskey collection in the western hemisphere, where more than 2600 bottles stack the infinite shelves.*

○ **Dan's Cafe (p134)** *Indulging in a squirt bottle of booze at one of DC's premier dive bars.*

○ **Madam's Organ (p134)** *Catching a blues band, drinking on the rooftop deck and snapping a photo of the bawdy mural outside.*

Getting There & Around

Ⓜ To reach most of 18th St, use the Woodley Park-Zoo/Adams Morgan station (Red Line). For points on 18th St south of Kalorama Rd, the Dupont Circle station (Red Line) is closer. Each station is about a 15-minute walk away.

🚌 The DC Circulator runs from the Woodley Park-Zoo/Adams Morgan Metro to the corner of 18th and Calvert Sts.

Neighborhood Map on p130

18th Street (p134) PHILIP SCALIA/ALAMY ©

Adams Morgan

15th St NW

Meridian Hill Park

MERIDIAN HILL

16th St NW

W St NW

Florida Ave NW

U St (0.3mi)

Mozart Pl NW

Euclid St NW

Crescent Pl NW

Belmont St NW

17th St NW

Kalorama Rd NW

V St NW

16th St NW

Ontario Rd NW

Champlain St NW

18th St NW

Seaton Pl NW

Columbia Rd NW

11 · 15 · 12 · 8
18th St NW

13 · 3 · 5
District of Columbia Arts Center · 1

6

10

U St NW

Lanier Pl NW

Adams Mill Rd NW

2

7 · 4

ADAMS MORGAN

Belmont Rd NW

Kalorama Rd NW

Wyoming Ave NW

California St NW

14

KALORAMA

9

Dupont Circle (0.4mi)

Calvert St NW

Biltmore St NW

Mintwood Pl NW

Kalorama Park

Columbia Rd NW

19th St NW

Waterside Dr NW

20th St NW

Kalorama Rd NW

200 m
0.1 miles

Woodley Park (0.3mi)

Connecticut Ave NW

For reviews see	
Sights	p131
Eating	p131
Drinking	p134
Entertainment	p134
Shopping	p135

Sights

District of Columbia Arts Center
ARTS CENTER

1 ◎ MAP P130, C2

The grassroots DCAC offers emerging artists a space to showcase their work. The 800-sq-ft gallery features rotating visual-arts exhibits, while plays, improv, avant-garde musicals and other theatrical productions take place in the 42-seat theater. The gallery is free and worth popping into to see what's showing. (DCAC; ☑202-462-7833; www.dcartscenter.org; 2438 18th St NW; admission free; ⏱2-7pm Wed-Sun; Ⓜ Red Line to Woodley Park-Zoo/Adams Morgan)

Eating

Tail Up Goat
MEDITERRANEAN $$

2 ✖ MAP P130, C1

With its pale-blue walls, light wood decor and lantern-like lights dangling overhead, Tail Up Goat exudes a warm, island-y vibe. The lamb ribs are the specialty – crispy and lusciously fatty, served with date-molasses juice. The house-made breads and spreads star on the menu too – say, flaxseed sourdough with beets. No wonder Michelin gave it a star. (☑202-986-9600; www.tailupgoat.com; 1827 Adams Mill Rd NW; mains $18-27; ⏱5:30-10pm Mon-Thu, 5-10pm Fri & Sat, 11am-1pm & 5-10pm Sun; Ⓜ Red Line to Woodley Park-Zoo/Adams Morgan)

BUL

This place (☑202-733-3921; www.buldc.com; 2431 18th St NW; mains $14-21; ⏱5:30-10:30pm Tue-Thu, to 2am Fri, 4:30pm-2am Sat, to 10pm Sun; Ⓜ Red Line to Woodley Park-Zoo/Adams Morgan) is DC's first *pojangmacha* ('covered wagon'), or Korean street-food eatery. Trendy locals love it, gobbling up grilled skewers of meat and vegetables, seafood pancakes, and a fishcakey 'hangover soup.' The pork belly fried rice comes with roasted kimchi made by the chefs' mothers.

Donburi
JAPANESE $

3 ✖ MAP P130, C2

Hole-in-the-wall Donburi has 14 seats at a wooden counter where you get a front-row view of the slicing, dicing chefs. *Donburi* means 'bowl' in Japanese, and that's what arrives steaming hot and filled with, say, panko-coated shrimp atop rice, blended with the house's sweet-and-savory sauce. It's a simple, authentic meal. There's often a line, but it moves quickly. No reservations. (☑202-629-1047; www.donburidc.com; 2438 18th St NW; mains $11-13; ⏱11am-10pm; Ⓜ Red Line to Woodley Park-Zoo/Adams Morgan)

Mintwood Place

AMERICAN $$

4 MAP P130, C2

In a neighborhood known for jumbo pizza slices and Jell-O shots, Mintwood Place is a romantic anomaly. Take a seat in a brown-leather booth or at a reclaimed-wood table under twinkling lights. Then sniff the French-American fusion dishes that emerge from the wood-burning oven. The *flammekueche* (onion and bacon tart), chicken-liver mousse and black-truffle-and-Parmesan risotto show how it's done. (✆202-234-6732; www.mintwoodplace.com; 1813 Columbia Rd NW; mains $18-28; ⏰5:30-10pm Tue-Thu, to 10:30pm Fri & Sat, to 9pm Sun, plus 10:30am-2:30pm Sat & Sun; Ⓜ Red Line to Woodley Park-Zoo/Adams Morgan)

Diner

AMERICAN $

5 MAP P130, C2

The Diner serves hearty comfort food, any time of the day or night. It's ideal for wee-hour breakfast scarf-downs, weekend Bloody Mary brunches (if you don't mind crowds) or any time you want unfussy, well-prepared American fare. Omelets, fat buttermilk pancakes, mac 'n' cheese, veggie tacos and burgers hit the tables with aplomb. It's a good spot for kids, too. (✆202-232-8800; www.dinerdc.com; 2453 18th St NW; mains $9-18; ⏰24hr; ♿🚼; Ⓜ Red Line to Woodley Park-Zoo/Adams Morgan)

Amsterdam Falafelshop

MIDDLE EASTERN $

6 MAP P130, D2

Cheap and cheerful, fast and delicious, the Falafelshop rocks the world of vegetarians and those questing for late-night munchies. Bowl up to the counter, order your falafel sandwich, then take it to the topping bar and pile on pickles, tabbouleh, olives and 20 other items. Take away, or dribble away at the scattering of stools and tables. (✆202-234-1969; www.falafelshop.com; 2425 18th St NW; items $6-8; ⏰11am-midnight Sun & Mon, to 2:30am Tue-Thu, to 4am Fri & Sat; ♿; Ⓜ Red Line to Woodley Park-Zoo/Adams Morgan)

Perry's

JAPANESE $$

7 MAP P130, C2

You can munch sushi at Perry's, but it's the creative fusion fare that really deserves your tongue's attention. Eat in the attractive lounge or under the stars on the rooftop. Sunday brings something entirely different: drag-queen brunch. The megapopular campy show plus buffet is a scene to behold. Make reservations (up to two months in advance). (✆202-234-6218; www.perrysam.com; 1811 Columbia Rd NW; mains $15-26; ⏰5:30-10pm Mon-Thu, to 11pm Fri & Sat, 10am-3pm & 5:30-10pm Sun; Ⓜ Red Line to Woodley Park-Zoo/Adams Morgan)

Al fresco dining at Tryst

Tryst
CAFE $

8 ⊗ MAP P130, C2

The couches, armchairs and bookshelves, and the light flooding through streetside windows, lure patrons so faithful they probably should pay rent at Tryst. They crowd in for the coffee, stellar omelet and waffle breakfasts, and creative sandwiches. Come night fall, baristas become bartenders, and the cafe hosts jazzy live music several nights a week. (☏202-232-5500; www.trystdc.com; 2459 18th St NW; breakfast & sandwiches $8-12; ☼7am-midnight Sun-Thu, to 1am Fri & Sat; ☎; Ⓜ Red Line to Woodley Park-Zoo/Adams Morgan)

CakeRoom
BAKERY $

9 ⊗ MAP P130, D4

Ogle the glass cases bursting with creamy-frosted cakes and pies. The banoffee pie (a sublime banana-toffee mix) and carrot cupcake are the sweets to beat. Fadi, the baker, is from Jordan, and he invites guests to linger on the comfy couches and armchairs upstairs in the old-timey shop. (☏202-450-4462; www.cakeroombakery.com; 2006 18th St NW; baked goods $2.50-5; ☼9am-9pm Mon-Thu, to 10pm Fri, 10am-10pm Sat, to 9pm Sun; ☎; Ⓜ Red Line to Dupont Circle)

Late-Night Bites

Adams Morgan is famed for its late-night eateries. Lots of people come here post-party on weekend nights to soak up the booze. Huge slices of pizza are a traditional snack: they're sold everywhere around the neighborhood and are uniformly greasy and delicious after several libations.

Drinking

Dan's Cafe BAR

10 🚇 MAP P130, D3

This is one of DC's great dive bars. The interior looks sort of like an evil Elks Club, all unironically old-school 'art,' cheap paneling and dim lights barely illuminating the unapologetic slumminess. It's famed for its whopping, mix-it-yourself drinks, where you get a ketchup-type squirt bottle of booze, a can of soda and bucket of ice for $20. Cash only. (📞202-265-0299; 2315 18th St NW; ⏰7pm-2am Tue-Thu, to 3am Fri & Sat; Ⓜ Red Line to Woodley Park-Zoo/Adams Morgan)

Songbyrd Record Cafe & Music House CAFE

11 🚇 MAP P130, C1

By day hang out in the retro cafe, drinking excellent coffee, munching sandwiches and browsing the soul and indie LPs for sale. You can even cut your own record in the vintage recording booth ($15). By night the party moves to the DJ-spinning bar, where beer and cocktails flow alongside burgers and tacos, and indie bands rock the basement club. (📞202-450-2917; www.songbyrddc.com; 2475-2477 18th St NW; mains $10-14; ⏰8am-2am Sun-Thu, to 3am Fri & Sat, cafe to 10pm; 📶; Ⓜ Red Line to Woodley Park-Zoo/Adams Morgan)

Entertainment

Madam's Organ LIVE MUSIC

12 ⭐ MAP P130, C2

Playboy magazine once named Madam's Organ one of its favorite bars in America. The ramshackle place has been around forever, and its nightly blues, rock and bluegrass shows can be downright riot-inducing. There's a raunchy bar-dancing scene and funky decor with stuffed animals and bizarre paintings on the 1st floor. The rooftop deck is more mellow. The big-boobed mural outside is a classic. (📞202-667-5370; www.madamsorgan.com; 2461 18th St NW; cover $5-10; ⏰5pm-2am Sun-Thu, to 3am Fri & Sat; Ⓜ Red Line to Woodley Park-Zoo/Adams Morgan)

Bukom Cafe LIVE MUSIC

13 ⭐ MAP P130, C2

Reggae and highlife bands take the stage nightly at Bukom. Be prepared for sore but happy hips as you join the mix of West African immigrants and ex–Peace Corps types who've earned their dancing

JONATHAN NEWTON/THE WASHINGTON POST VIA GETTY IMAGES ©

Madam's Organ

chops on the continent. The music starts at 10pm (earlier weekdays); there's no cover charge. Come early and sample the chicken *yassa* and other West African fare. (📞202-265-4600; 2442 18th St NW; ⊗4:30pm-2am; Ⓜ Red Line to Woodley Park-Zoo/Adams Morgan)

Shopping

Meeps   VINTAGE

14 Ⓐ MAP P130, C4

There's this girl you know: extremely stylish and never seems to have a brand name on her body. Now, picture her wardrobe. Mod dresses, cowboy shirts, suede jackets, beaded purses, leather boots, Jackie O sunglasses and denim jumpsuits: that's Meeps mapped out for you. The store also

carries a selection of clever, locally designed T-shirts. (📞202-265-6546; www.meepsdc.com; 2104 18th St NW; ⊗noon-7pm Sun & Mon, to 8pm Tue-Sat; Ⓜ Red Line to Dupont Circle)

Idle Time Books   BOOKS

15 Ⓐ MAP P130, C2

Three creaky floors are stuffed with secondhand literature and non-fiction, including one of the best secondhand political and history collections in the city. Its sci-fi, sports and humor sections are top-notch, and there's a good newsstand in its front window. (📞202-232-4774; www.idletimebooks.com; 2467 18th St NW; ⊗11am-10pm; Ⓜ Red Line to Woodley Park-Zoo/Adams Morgan)

Walking Tour 🥾

Mixing It Up in Columbia Heights

Columbia Heights booms with Latino immigrants and hipsters. A few decades ago the neighborhood was a tumbledown mess. Then the Metro station was built, followed by a slew of big-box retailers. And then – this is why you're here – it morphed into a cool-cat mix of ethnic restaurants and unassuming corner taverns chock-full of local color.

Start Columbia Heights Metro Station

Finish Meridian Pint

Length 1 mile

Metro Green or Yellow Line to Columbia Heights.

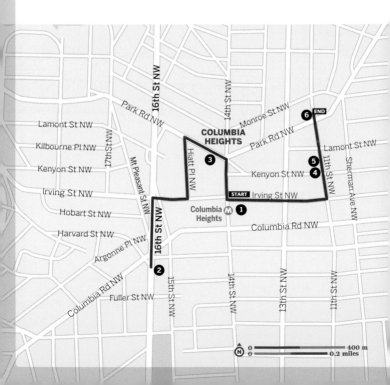

❶ Catalyst for Change

The arrival of a Metro station to Columbia Heights in recent decades was a catalyst for development in this now very hip neighborhood. Start your tour there - it's become one of the busiest stops outside downtown.

❷ Mexican Cultural Institute

The **Mexican Cultural Institute** (www.instituteofmexicodc.org; 2829 16th St NW, Columbia Heights; admission free; ⊙10am-6pm Mon-Fri, noon-4pm Sat) looks imposing, but don't be deterred. The gilded beaux-arts mansion is open to the public and hosts excellent art and cultural exhibitions. Ring the doorbell for entry.

❸ Los Hermanos

When Dominican baseball players come to town to play the Nats, **Los Hermanos** (www.loshermanosfordc.com; 1426-8 Park Rd NW; mains $10-14; ⊙10am-9pm Mon-Sat, to 8pm Sun) is where they get their food fix. It's cafeteria-style service, so head to the counter, point to what you want behind the glass – maybe pork *mofongo* (fried green plantains) or stewed oxtail.

❹ Wonderland Ballroom

Divey **Wonderland Ballroom** (www.thewonderlandballroom.com; 1101 Kenyon St NW; ⊙5pm-2am Mon-Thu, 4pm-3am Fri, 11am-3pm Sat, from 10am Sun) flaunts a spacious patio with outsized wooden benches that are just right on warm evenings. The upstairs dance floor sees a mix of DJs and bands, and is packed on weekends. The interior is clapped out in vintage signs and could be a folk-art museum.

❺ BloomBars

You never know what you'll find going on at **BloomBars** (www.bloombars.com; 3222 11th St NW; by donation; ⊙hours vary), a cool community arts center. By day, children's story times and music classes take place. At night, gallery shows and indie movie screenings.

❻ Meridian Pint

Staffed by locals, **Meridian Pint** (www.meridianpint.com; 3400 11th St NW; ⊙5pm-midnight Mon-Thu, to 3am Fri, 10am-3am Sat, from 10am Sun;) is the quintessential corner tavern for Columbia Heights. Strings of lights twinkle overhead, sports flicker on TV, folks play pool and shuffleboard, and impressive American craft beers flow.

Worth a Trip 🔭
Visit JFK's Grave at Arlington National Cemetery

At the US's national military cemetery, simple white headstones mark the sacrifice of more than 400,000 service members and their dependents. The 624-acre grounds contain the dead of every war the US has fought since the Revolution. Still in active use, it's not uncommon to see families gathered around flag-draped caskets or hear a lone bugle's heartrending lament.

www.arlingtoncemetery.mil

admission free

🕙 8am-7pm Apr-Sep, to 5pm Oct-Mar

Ⓜ Blue Line to Arlington Cemetery

Tomb of the Unknowns

The **Tomb of the Unknown Soldier** (off Wilson Dr, Arlington National Cemetery) contains the remains of unidentified US service members from both world wars and the Korean War. A special military unit of white-gloved, rifle-toting sentinels maintains a round-the-clock vigil. The changing of the guard (every hour October through March, every half hour April through September) is one of Arlington's most moving sights.

Kennedy Gravesites

An eternal flame marks the grave of **John F Kennedy** (off Sheridan Dr, Arlington National Cemetery), next to those of Jacqueline Kennedy Onassis and their two children who died in infancy. Stones of Cape Cod granite pave the area; the clover and sedum growing in the crevices are meant to evoke a Massachusetts field. JFK's brother Bobby is buried 100ft southwest along the path. Youngest brother Ted also lies nearby.

Arlington House

Much of the cemetery was built on the grounds of **Arlington House** (🕿703-235-1530; www.nps. gov/arho; Sherman Dr, Arlington National Cemetery; admission free; ⏱10am-4pm), the former home of Robert E Lee and his wife Mary Anna Custis Lee. The interior of the handsome Greek Revival mansion can be visited, but is unfurnished and in sore need of restoration.

Other Memorials

The Space Shuttle Challenger Memorial is near the Tomb of the Unknown Soldier. The USS Maine Memorial, is also nearby. A bit further on is the controversial **Confederate Memorial** (off McPherson Dr, Arlington National Cemetery; Ⓜ Blue Line to Arlington Cemetery) that honors war dead from the Civil War's breakaway states.

★ **Top Tips**

○ Pick up a free cemetery map at the cemetery's Welcome Center.

○ Hop-on, hop-off bus tours (adult/child $13.50/6.75) are an easy way to hit the highlights.

○ You can download the excellent free ANC Explorer app onto your phone.

○ Arlington is near the Lincoln and Vietnam memorials, so they're easy to visit next.

✗ **Take a Break**

Ireland's Four Courts (www.irelands fourcourts.com; 2051 Wilson Blvd; ⏱11am-2am Mon-Fri, 8am-2am Sat & Sun) brings on the Guinness and shepherd's pie in classic pub style. It's 2 miles NW of the cemetery.

★ **Getting There**

Ⓜ Blue Line to Arlington Cemetery. Though Arlington is in Virginia, it's only a few stops southwest of the National Mall.

Survival Guide

Before You Go 142

Book Your Stay 142

When to Go 142

Arriving in Washington, DC 143

From Ronald Reagan Washington
National Airport 143

From Washington Dulles International Airport 143

From Union Station 144

Getting Around 144

Metro 144

Bus 144

Taxi & Ride Share 144

Bicycle 145

Car & Motorcycle 145

Essential Information 145

Accessible Travel 145

Business Hours 146

COVID-19 Requirements 146

Electricity 146

LGBTIQ+ Travellers 147

Money 147

Public Holidays 147

Responsible Travel 147

Telephone 148

Tourist Information 148

Visas 149

Union Station (p144) KAMIRA/SHUTTERSTOCK ©

Before You Go

Book Your Stay

o The White House area, downtown and Dupont Circle are the most lodging-filled neighborhoods.

o Washington's 14.5% hotel tax is not included in most quoted rates.

o For parking costs, figure on $35 to $55 per day for in-and-out privileges.

Useful Websites

Lonely Planet (www.lonelyplanet.com/usa/washington-dc/hotels) Recommendations and author reviews.

Bed & Breakfast DC (www.bedandbreakfastdc.com) One-stop shop for booking B&Bs and apartments.

WDCA Hotels (www.wdcahotels.com) Discounter that sorts by neighborhood, price or ecofriendliness.

Destination DC (www.washington.org) Options from the tourism office's jam-packed website.

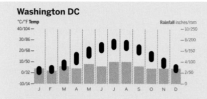

When to Go

o **Winter** (Dec–Feb) December is festive. January booms if it's an inauguration year. Otherwise, low season bargains abound. Gray and chilly.

o **Spring** (Mar–May) Peak tourism season thanks to cherry blossoms and school-group visits. Comfy weather.

o **Summer** (Jun–Aug) Busy with summer holiday crowds, lots of festivals. Hot, humid, 90-degree-plus temperatures.

o **Autumn** (Sep–Nov) Fewer tourists but business travelers keep hotel rates high. Cooler weather; trees burst with color.

Best Budget

Adam's Inn (www.adamsinn.com) Twenty-seven rooms to make yourself at home, in a couple of Adams Morgan townhouses.

Hostelling International – Washington DC (www.hiwashingtondc.org) Big, amenity-laden hostel that draws a laid-back international crowd.

William Penn House (www.williampennhouse.org) Quaker-run guesthouse with garden and dorms.

HighRoad Hostel (www.highroadhostels.com) Modern dorms and upscale amenities near Adams Morgan's nightlife.

Best Midrange

Hotel Lombardy (www.hotellombardy.com) International types tuck into handsome, antique-laden rooms.

Tabard Inn (www.tab-ardinn.com) Offbeat, TV-less rooms set in cozy Victorian row houses.

Chester A Arthur House (www.chesterar-thurhouse.com) Logan Circle manor stuffed with chandeliers, oriental rugs and character.

Kimpton Carlyle (www.carlylehoteldc.com) Oft-overlooked, art-deco beauty sitting amid Dupont Circle's embassies.

Cambria Washington DC Convention Center (www.cambriadc.com) Shiny new ecofriendly building with vast rooms and near the Convention Center.

Best Top End

Hay-Adams Hotel (www.hayadams.com) Old-school luxury a stone's throw from the White House.

The Jefferson (www.jeffersondc.com) Luxurious, romantic, Parisian and often considered DC's top address.

Willard InterContinental Hotel (www.wash-ington.intercontinental.com) When visiting heads of state come to town, they snooze in the Willard's gilded suites.

St Regis Washington (www.stregiswashing-tondc.com) Built to look like an Italian grand palace, with rooms opulent enough for nobility.

Arriving in Washington, DC

From Ronald Reagan Washington National Airport

o **Metro** The airport has its own Metro station (www.wmata.com) on the Blue and Yellow Lines. Trains (around $2.60) depart every 10 minutes or so between 5am and midnight (to 3am Friday and Saturday); they reach the city center in 20 minutes.

o **Shuttle van** The Supershuttle (www.supershuttle.com) door-to-door shared van service goes downtown for $16. It takes 10 to 30 minutes and runs from 5:30am to 12:30am.

o **Taxi** Rides to the city center take 10 to 30 minutes (depending on traffic) and cost $15 to $22. Taxis queue outside the baggage-claim area at each terminal.

From Washington Dulles International Airport

o **Bus & Metro** Washington Flyer's (www.washfly.com) Silver Line Express bus runs every 15 to 20 minutes from Dulles (main terminal, arrivals level door 4) to the Wiehle-Reston East Metro station between 6am and 10:40pm (from 7:45am weekends). Total time to DC's center is 60 to 75 minutes, total bus-Metro tickets cost around $11.

o **Bus** Metrobus 5A (www.wmata.com) runs every 30 to 40 minutes from Dulles to Rosslyn Metro (Blue, Orange and Silver Lines) and on to central DC (L'Enfant Plaza) between 5:50am (6:30am weekends) and 11:35pm.

o Total time to the center is around 60 minutes; total fare is $7.

○ Shuttle van The Supershuttle (www. supershuttle.com) door-to-door shared van service goes downtown for $30. It takes 30 to 60 minutes and runs from 5:30am to 12:30am.

○ Taxi Rides to the city center take 30 to 60 minutes (depending on traffic) and cost $62 to $73.

From Union Station

○ Metro There's a Metro (Red Line) stop inside Union Station for easy onward transport. The station is a few stops northeast of downtown.

○ Taxi Taxis queue outside the main entrance. A ride to downtown costs around $7, to Dupont Circle $10.

Getting Around

Metro

○ DC's modern subway network is the Metrorail (www.wmata.com), commonly called Metro.

○ Trains start running at 5am Monday through Friday (from 7am on weekends); the last service is around midnight Sunday through Thursday and 3am on Friday and Saturday.

○ There are six color-coded lines: Red, Orange, Blue, Green, Yellow and Silver.

○ Fare cards are called SmarTrip cards. Machines inside all stations sell them. The plastic, rechargeable card costs $10, with $8 of that stored for fares. You then add value as needed.

○ Fares cost $1.85 to $6, depending on distance traveled and time of day. Fares increase slightly during morning and evening rush hour.

○ Use the card to enter *and* exit station turnstiles. Upon exit, the turnstile deducts the fare and opens the gate. If the value of the card is insufficient, you need to use an 'Addfare' machine to add money.

Bus

○ DC's public bus system has two main fleets: Circulator and Metrobus.

○ DC Circulator (www. dccirculator.com) buses run along handy local routes, including Union Station to/from the Mall (looping by all major museums and memorials), Union Station to/from Georgetown (via K St), Dupont Circle to/from Georgetown (via M St), and the White House area to/from Adams Morgan (via 14th St).

○ Circulator buses operate from roughly 7am to 9pm weekdays (midnight or so on weekends). Fare is $1.

○ Metrobus (www. wmata.com) operates throughout the city and suburbs, typically from early morning until late evening. Fare is $2.

○ Pay with exact change, or use a SmarTrip card for all buses.

Taxi & Ride Share

○ Taxis queue at Union Station, the main hotels and sports venues, but it's not always easy to hail one on the street.

○ Fares are meter-based. The meter starts at $3.25, then it's $2.16 per mile thereafter.

○ There's a $2 surcharge for telephone dispatches. Try DC Yellow Cab (202-544-1212) if you need a pickup.

o Ride-hailing companies Uber (www.uber.com), Lyft (www.lyft.com) and Via (www.ridewithvia.com) are popular in the District. Locals say they save time and money compared to taxis.

Bicycle

o Capital Bikeshare

(☎877-430-2453; www.capitalbikeshare.com; per 1/3 days $8/17) has 3700-plus bicycles scattered at 440-odd stations, including many that fringe the Mall.

o Kiosks issue passes (one day or three days) on the spot. Insert a credit card, get your ride code, then unlock a bike.

o The first 30 minutes are free; after that, rates rise fast if you don't dock the bike.

o There's also an option for a 'single trip' ($2), ie a one-off ride of under 30 minutes.

o Bike rentals for longer rides (with accoutrements such as helmets and locks) start at $16 per two hours. Try **Bike & Roll** (☎202-842-2453; www.bikeandrolldc.com; 955 L'Enfant Plaza SW,

Dos & Don'ts

o **Smoking** Don't smoke in restaurants or bars: DC is smoke free by law in those venues.

o **Dining** People eat dinner early in Washington, often by 6pm.

o **On the Metro** Stand to the right on the escalators; walk on the left.

o **Conversation** It's OK to ask locals you've just met, 'What do you do for work?' Most people in DC have an intriguing job that they're happy to discuss.

South DC; tours adult/child from $44/34; ⊘9am-8pm, reduced hours spring & fall, closed early Jan–mid-Mar; Ⓜ Orange, Silver, Blue, Yellow, Green Line to L'Enfant Plaza) or **Big Wheel Bikes** (☎202-337-0254; www.bigwheelbikes.com; 1034 33rd St NW; per 3hr/day $21/35; ⊘11am-7pm Tue-Fri, 10am-6pm Sat & Sun; 🚌 Circulator).

Car & Motorcycle

o Avoid driving in DC. Traffic is constant, and street parking is scarce.

o Parking garages in the city cost $15 to $35 per day.

o Clogged rush-hour streets in DC include the main access arteries from the suburbs: Massachusetts, Wisconsin, Connecticut and Geor-

gia Aves NW, among others.

Essential Information

Accessible Travel

o Most museums and major sights are wheelchair accessible, as are most large hotels and restaurants.

o All Metro trains and buses are accessible to people in wheelchairs. All Metro stations have elevators, and guide dogs are allowed on trains and buses.

o All DC transit companies offer travel discounts for disabled travelers.

o Hindrances to wheel-

Money-Saving Tips

● Make the most of DC's abundant free sights and entertainment.

● Take advantage of happy hour, when bars have drink and/or food specials for a few hours between 4pm and 7pm.

● Unlimited-ride Metro day passes cost $14.50, available at any station.

chair users include buckled-brick sidewalks in the historic blocks of Georgetown and Capitol Hill, but sidewalks in most other parts of DC are in good shape.

● All Smithsonian museums have free wheelchair loans and can arrange special tours for hearing-impaired visitors. See www.si.edu/Visit/VisitorsWithDisabilities for more. Download Lonely Planet's free Accessible Travel guide from https://shop.lonelyplanet.com/categories/accessible-travel

Business Hours

Typical opening times in Washington, DC, are as follows:

Bars 5pm to 1am or 2am weekdays, 3am on weekends

Museums 10am to 5:30pm

Nightclubs 9pm to 1am or 2am weekdays, 3am or 4am on weekends

Offices & Government Agencies 9am to 5pm Monday to Friday

Restaurants Breakfast 7am or 8am to 11am; lunch 11am or 11:30am to 2:30pm; dinner 5pm or 6pm to 10pm Sunday to Thursday, to 11pm or midnight Friday and Saturday

Shops 10am to 7pm Monday to Saturday, noon to 6pm Sunday

COVID-19 Requirements

● COVID-19 travel protocols are subject to change. For updated information on requirements for travel to/within the US, visit the CDC website (www.cdc.gov/coronavirus) and www.canitravel.net.

● Current COVID-19 protocols for Washington, DC can be found at www.coronavirus.dc.gov. Some indoor venues may require proof of vaccination to enter.

Electricity

LGBTIQ+ Travelers

Washington DC is a progressive, liberally minded city with thriving communities across the spectrum of sexual and gender identities; estimates suggest that the city has the highest population percentage of people who identify as a member of the broader LGBTIQ+ community in the United States.

While LGBTIQ+ people may face discriminatory attitudes, as they might elsewhere in the US, the city's population as a whole is known for generally welcoming attitudes toward sexual orientations and gender identities.

Money

ATMs

o ATMs are available 24/7 at banks, airports and convenience shops.

o Most ATMs link into worldwide networks (Plus, Cirrus, Exchange etc).

o ATMs typically charge a service fee of $3 or more per transaction.

Credit Cards

o Visa, MasterCard and American Express are widely accepted at hotels, restaurants, bars and shops.

Tipping

Tipping is not optional. Only withhold tips in cases of outrageously bad service.

o **Airport & hotel porters** $2 per bag, minimum per cart $5

o **Bartenders** 15% to 20% per round, minimum $1 per drink for standard drinks, $2 per specialty cocktail

o **Housekeeping staff** $2 to $5 per night

o **Restaurant servers** 18% to 20%, unless a gratuity is already charged on the bill

o **Taxi drivers** 10% to 15%, rounded up to the next dollar

o **Parking valets** $2 to $5 when you're handed back the keys

Public Holidays

Banks, schools, offices and most shops close on these days.

New Year's Day January 1

Martin Luther King Jr Day Third Monday in January

Inauguration Day January 20, every four years

Presidents' Day Third Monday in February

Emancipation Day April 16

Memorial Day Last Monday in May

Independence Day July 4

Labor Day First Monday in September

Columbus Day Second Monday in October

Veterans Day November 11

Thanksgiving Day Fourth Thursday in November

Christmas Day December 25

Responsible Travel

Overtourism

o Travel off-season: outside of the late March through June peak period, and midweek instead of weekends.

o Stay in registered

accommodation. Illegal rentals drive up housing prices for locals. The city's website (https://dcra.dc.gov/short-termrentals) lets you search your address to see if it's licensed.

Support Local & Give Back

o DC Shop Small (www.dcshopsmall.com) lists local small businesses selling art, clothing, homewares, books, food and more.

o Help restore wetlands, collect seeds and protect mussels with the Anacostia Watershed Society (www.anacostiaws.org); the events calendar has project listings.

o Prepare meals and sort and pack food donations with the Capital Area Food Bank (www.capitalareafoodbank.org) and DC Central Kitchen (www.dccentralkitchen.org).

o Plant and care for maples, magnolias and more with Casey Trees (www.caseytrees.org) as it enhances the tree canopy throughout the city.

Leave a Light Footprint

o Make use of DC's public transportation network; goDCgo (www.godcgo.com) has the lowdown on travel by bus, train, bike, scooter and foot.

o Bicycles are a particular favorite for getting around.

o Join locals using the Capital Bikeshare (www.capitalbikeshare.com) program in neighborhoods citywide.

o Check the DC Sustainability Guide (www.washington.org/sustainability) for ecofriendly hotels, attractions and eateries.

Telephone

US country code 1

DC area code 202

Making international calls Dial 011 + country code + area code + local number.

Calling other US area codes or Canada Dial 1 + area code + seven-digit local number.

Calling within DC Dial the seven-digit local number. If for some reason it doesn't work, try adding 1 then the area code at the beginning.

Toilets

There are public toilets near most of the major monuments and memorials. The many museums also offer public restrooms for their visitors. You'll find public toilets in shopping malls and public parks. They are generally free of charge. If you're in a pinch, buy something in one of the city's many coffee shops or bars and use their facilities.

Tourist Information

o Destination DC is DC's official tourism site, and the mother lode of online information.

o **Smithsonian Visitor Center** (Map p46, F4; ☏202-663-1000; www.si.edu/visit; 1000 Jefferson Dr SW; ⊙8:30am-5:30pm; 🛜; 🚌Circulator, MOrange, Silver, Blue Line to Smithsonian) Located in the Castle, it is a great resource with a staffed information desk and everything you ever wanted to know about the museum programs.

Visas

The Visa Waiver Program (VWP) allows nationals from some 38 countries (including most EU countries, Japan, Australia and New Zealand) to enter the US without a visa for up to 90 days.

VWP visitors require an e-passport (with electronic chip) and approval under the Electronic System For Travel Authorization at least three days before arrival.

There is a $21 fee for processing and authorization (payable online). Once approved, the registration is valid for two years.

Those who need a visa – ie anyone staying longer than 90 days, or from a non-VWP country – should apply at the US consulate in their home country.

Check with the US Department of State (www.travel.state.gov) for updates and details on entry requirements. For specific information on COVID-19 protocols for travel to the US, visit the CDC website (www.cdc.gov/coronavirus) and www.canitravel.net.

Behind the Scenes

Send Us Your Feedback

We love to hear from travelers – your comments help make our books better. We read every word, and we guarantee that your feedback goes straight to the authors. Visit **lonelyplanet.com/contact** to submit your updates and suggestions.

Note: We may edit, reproduce and incorporate your comments in Lonely Planet products such as guidebooks, websites and digital products, so let us know if you are happy to have your name acknowledged. For a copy of our privacy policy visit **lonelyplanet.com/legal**.

Karla's Thanks

Deep appreciation to all of the locals who spilled the beans on their favorite places. Thanks most to Eric Markowitz, the world's best partner-for-life, who kindly indulges my Abe Lincoln fixation. You top my Best List.

Acknowledgements

Front cover photograph:
Capitol Building Wasington DC,

lunamarina/Shutterstock ©

Back cover photograph:
Smithsonian National Air and Space Museum, Anna Krivitskaya/Shutterstock ©.

Climate map data adapted from Peel MC, Finlayson BL & McMahon TA (2007) 'Updated World Map of the Köppen-Geiger Climate Classification', Hydrology and Earth System Sciences, 11, 1633–44.

This Book

This 4th edition of Lonely Planet's *Pocket Washington, DC* guidebook was curated, researched and written by Karla Zimmerman. The previous editions were written by Karla Zimmerman and Adam Karlin.

This guidebook was produced by the following:

Commissioning Editor
Kirsten Rawlings
Product Editor
Gary Quinn
Cartographer
Corey Hutchison

Book Designer
Clara Monitto
Cover Researcher
Hannah Blackie
Thanks to Ronan Abayawickrema, Sonia Kapoor, Alison Killilea, Gabrielle Stefanos

Index

See also separate subindexes for:

- ⊗ **Eating** p153
- 🍷 **Drinking** p154
- 🎭 **Entertainment** p154
- 🛍 **Shopping** p154

A

accessible travel 145-146
accommodations 142-3
activities 24, 25, see also individual activities
Adams Morgan 129-35, **130**
  drinking 134
  entertainment 134
  food 131-3
  shopping 135
  sights 131
  transportation 129
African American Civil War Memorial 24
airports 143-4
Anderson House 127
architecture 22, 126-7
Arlington National Cemetery 9, 138-139
art 22, 117
atms 147

B

bathrooms 148

Sights 000
Map Pages **000**

beer 16
bicycling 25, 76, 90, 145
Big Wheel Bikes 76
Bike & Roll 90
Blaine Mansion 127
Book Hill Antiques 73
books 17
Brookland 24
Booth, John Wilkes 110
Bureau of Engraving & Printing 91
bus travel 144
business hours 146

C

C&O Canal Towpath 75
Capital Crescent Trail 76
Capital Pride 20
Capitol Hill 81-94, **88-9**
  drinking 93-5
  entertainment 95
  food 91-3
  history 94
  sights 90-1
  transportation 81
  walking tour 86-7, **86**
car travel 145
cell phones 28
children, travel with 14-15
Chinatown 104
cinema (Imax) 44
climate 142
cocktails 16
Columbia Heights 24, 136-7, **137**
comedy 21
costs 28, 147
COVID 19 3, 146
credit cards 147
Croatian Embassy 127
currency 28
cycling 25, 76, 90, 145

D

Daughters of the American Revolution Museum 65
Declaration of Independence 6
disabilities, travelers with 145-6
District of Columbia Arts Center 131
Douglass, Fredrick 94
Downtown, Penn Quarter & Logan Circle 97-111, **102-3**
  drinking 108
  entertainment 109-11

food 106-8
  history 110
  shopping 111
  sights 104-5
  transportation 97
drinking 16 see also individual neighborhoods, Drinking subindex
Dumbarton Oaks 25, 75
Dupont Circle 115-25
  drinking 123-5
  entertainment 125
  food 121-3
  shopping 125
  sights 120
  transportation 115
  walking tour 116
Dupont Underground 117

E

electricity 146
Ellipse 64
embassies 126-7
Embassy Row 120
entertainment 21, see also individual neighborhoods, Entertainment subindex
Nationals Park 95
National Theatre 21, 111

Shakespeare Theatre Company 109
Studio Theatre 111
etiquette 145
Exorcist Stairs 76

F

film locations 73, 76
films 14
Foggy Bottom 57
food 10-11
food trucks 65
Ford's Theatre 104
Foundry Gallery 113
Franklin Delano Roosevelt Memorial 52
Fridge 87

G

gay travelers 20, 147
Georgetown 71-9, **74**
  entertainment 78
  food 77-8
  sights 75-7
  walking tour 72-3, **72**
Georgetown University 76
Georgetown Waterfront Park 73

H

highlights 4-9
history 23, 68, 94, 110
holidays 147
Holocaust Memorial Museum 84-5
Howard Theatre 113

Sights 000
Map Pages **000**

I

Indonesian Embassy 127
International Spy Museum 104
itineraries 26-7

J

jazz 18, 112-113
Jefferson Memorial 51
JFK's grave 138

K

kayaking 25
Kenilworth Aquatic Gardens 24
Kennedy Center 67-9
Key Bridge Boathouse 75-6
Korean War Veterans Memorial 24

L

language 28
LGBTIQ+ travelers 20, 147
Library of Congress 90
Lincoln, Abraham 110
Lincoln assassination 110
Lincoln Memorial 36-7, 55
live music 18
Logan Circle, see Downtown, Penn Quarter & Logan Circle
Luxembourg Embassy 127

M

markets 17
Martin Luther King

Jr Memorial 48-9, 55
Mexican Cultural Institute 137
money 146, 147
monuments 12-13, 24
motorcycle travel 145
Mount Vernon Trail 76
museums 12-13, 19, 24
music 18

N

National Air & Space Museum 7, 42-4, 55
National Archives 98
National Building Museum 104-5
National Gallery of Art 49, 55
National Geographic Museum 120
National Mall 35-53, **46, 54**
  entertainment 53
  food 52-3
  history 50
  sights 53
  transportation 35
  walking tour 54-5, **55**
National Museum of African American History & Culture 48
National Museum of African Art 24
National Museum of American History 49
National Museum of Asian Art 51
National Museum of Natural History 49
National Museum

of the American Indian 52
National Museum of Women in the Arts 105
National Postal Museum 90
National Public Radio 91
National Sculpture Garden 53
National Theatre 111
National WWII Memorial 51

O

Old Stone House 77
opening hours 146

P

Penn Quarter, see Downtown, Penn Quarter & Logan Circle
Phillips Collection 120
politics 23
public holidays 147

R

Reflecting Pool 37, 46
Renwick Gallery 64
responsible travel 147
Reynolds Center for American Art & Portraiture 9, 13, 100-1
  ride sharing 144-5

S

Shaw 112-13, **112**
Sheridan Circle 127
shopping 15, 17, see also individual neighborhoods,

Shopping subindex
Smithson, James 45
Smithsonian 12, 45
Space Shuttle Challenger Memorial 139
Spanish Steps 127
stage 21
street art 87
Studio Gallery 120
subway travel 144
Supreme Court 90

T

taxis 144-5
telephone services 148
Textile Museum 64
theater 21
tickets 25
time 28
tipping 28, 147
toilets 148
Touchstone Gallery 22, 105-6
tourist information 148
transportation 29, 143-5
Tudor Place 24, 76-7
Turkish Ambassador's Residence 127

U

U Street 112-13, **112**
Union Station 144
United States National Arboretum 24
US Capitol 82

V

vacations 147
Verizon Center 25
Vietnam Veterans Memorial 38-9, 55
visas 28, 149

W

walks
  Capitol Hill 86-7, **86**
  Columbia Heights 136-7, **136**
  Dupont Circle 116-17, 126-7, **116**, **126**
  Embassy Row 126-7, **126**
  Georgetown 72-3, **72**
  National Mall 54-5, **55**
  U Street & Shaw 112-13, **112**
Washington Monument 5, 40-1, 55
Watergate Complex 64
weather 142
websites 142
White House 8, 55, 58-61
White House Area & Foggy Bottom 57-69, **62**
  drinking 66-7
  entertainment 67-9
  food 66
  history 68
  shopping 69
  sights 64-5
  transportation 57

Y

Yards Park 25

⊗ Eating

A

A Baked Joint 106
Ambar 87
Amsterdam Falafelshop 132

B

Baked & Wired 73
Ben's Chilli Bowl 11, 113
Birch & Barley 109
Bistrot du Coin 117
Blue Duck Tavern 123
Bub & Pop's 121
Bul 131

C

Cafe Milano 78
CakeRoom 133-4
Cascade Café 53
Central Michel Richard 106
Chercher 106-7
Chez Billy Sud 78

D

Dabney 10, 106
Diner 132
Dolcezza (Dupont Circle) 117
Dolcezza (Hirsh-horn) 41
Donburi 131
Dupont Circle Market 125
Duke's Grocery 117

E

El Sol 108
Ethiopic 91

F

Fiola Mare 77
Founding Farmers 66

G

Good Stuff Eatery 92-3

H

Hank's Oyster Bar 123

I

Ireland's Four Courts 139
Il Canale 77

L

Le Diplomate 107
Le Grenier 92
Little Serow 121
Los Hermanos 137

M

Maine Avenue Fish Market 92
Maple 137
Marcel's 66
Matchbox Vintage Pizza Bistro 108
Mintwood Place 132
Mitsitam Native Foods Cafe 52

O

Obelisk 121-2
Old Ebbitt Grill 66
Oohh's & Aahh's 113

P

Patisserie Poupon 73
Pavilion Cafe 53

Perry's 132
Pineapple & Pearls 92

R

Rasika 107
Red Apron Butchery 99
Rose's Luxury 87

S

Shouk 107
Simply Banh Mi 77
St Arnold's Mussel Bar 123

T

Tail Up Goat 131
Ted's Bulletin 92
Toki Underground 91
Tryst 133
Tune Inn 87

U

Union Market 11
Un Je Ne Sais Quoi 122

Z

Zaytinya 107
Zorba's Cafe 122

🍷 Drinking

18th Street Lounge 124

B

Bar Charley 123-4

Bardo Brewing 95
Bier Baron Tavern 124-5
Bluejacket Brewery 93-5

C

Cafe Bonaparte 78
Ching Ching Cha 78
Churchkey 108-9
Columbia Room 109
Copycat Co 93

D

Dacha Beer Garden 108
Dan's Cafe 134
Decades 124

F

Filter 124
Firefly Bar 124

G

Grace St Coffee 79
Granville Moore's 95

H

Hotel Hive 37

J

JR's 117

L

Larry's Lounge 20
Little Miss Whiskey's Golden Dollar 95

M

Madam's Organ 134
Martin's Tavern 73
Meridian Pint 137

O

Off the Record 66-7

R

Right Proper Brewing Co 113
Round Robin 67

S

Songbyrd Record Cafe & Music House 134

T

Tabard Inn Bar 117
Tombs 73

⭐ Entertainment

B

BloomBars 137
Blues Alley 78
Board Room 117
Bukom Cafe 134-5
Busboys & Poets 113

C

Capital One Arena 111

D

DC Improv 125
Discovery Theater 53

F

Ford's Theatre 104, 110

H

Hamilton 69
Howard Theatre 113

J

Jazz in the Garden 53

K

Kennedy Center 21, 67-9

N

Nationals Park 95
National Theatre 21, 111

S

Shakespeare Theatre Company 109

U

U St Music Hall 113

W

Wonderland Ballroom 137
Woolly Mammoth Theatre Company 21, 111

🛍 Shopping

Books 117
Capitol Hill Books 87
CityCenterDC 111
Eastern Market 87
Flea Market 87
Idle Time Books 135
Kramerbooks 117
Meeps 135
Oliver Dunn, Moss & Co 78-9
Second Story Books 125
Tabletop 125
Tugooh Toys 79

Sights 000
Map Pages **000**

Notes

CREDIT

CREDIT

Our Writer

Karla Zimmerman

Karla lives in Chicago, where she eat doughnuts, yells at the Cubs, and writes stuff for books, magazines, and websites when she's not doing the first two things. She has contributed to 40-plus guidebooks and travel anthologies covering destinations in Europe, Asia, Africa, North America, and the Caribbean – all of which are a long way from the early days, when she wrote about gravel for a construction magazine and got to trek to places like Fredonia, Kansas. To learn more, follow her on Instagram and Twitter (@karlazimmerman).

Published by Lonely Planet Global Limited
CRN 554153
4th edition – December 2022
ISBN 9781787016286
© Lonely Planet 2022 Photographs © as indicated 2022
10 9 8 7 6 5 4 3 2 1
Printed in Singapore